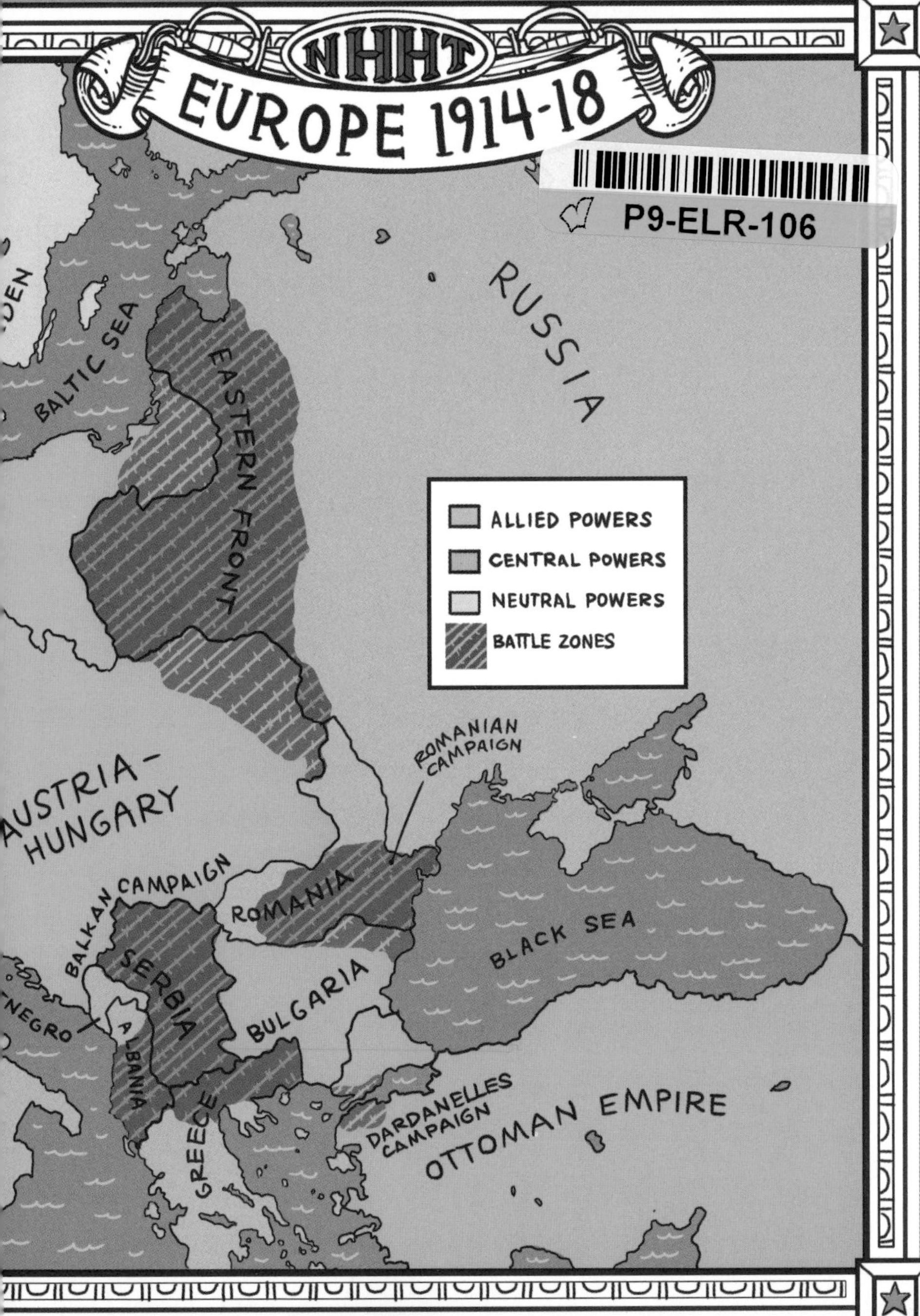
NHHT
EUROPE 1914-18
P9-ELR-106
RUSSIA
BALTIC SEA
EASTERN FRONT
ALLIED POWERS
CENTRAL POWERS
NEUTRAL POWERS
BATTLE ZONES
ROMANIAN CAMPAIGN
AUSTRIA-HUNGARY
BALKAN CAMPAIGN
ROMANIA
BLACK SEA
SERBIA
BULGARIA
ALBANIA
GREECE
DARDANELLES CAMPAIGN
OTTOMAN EMPIRE

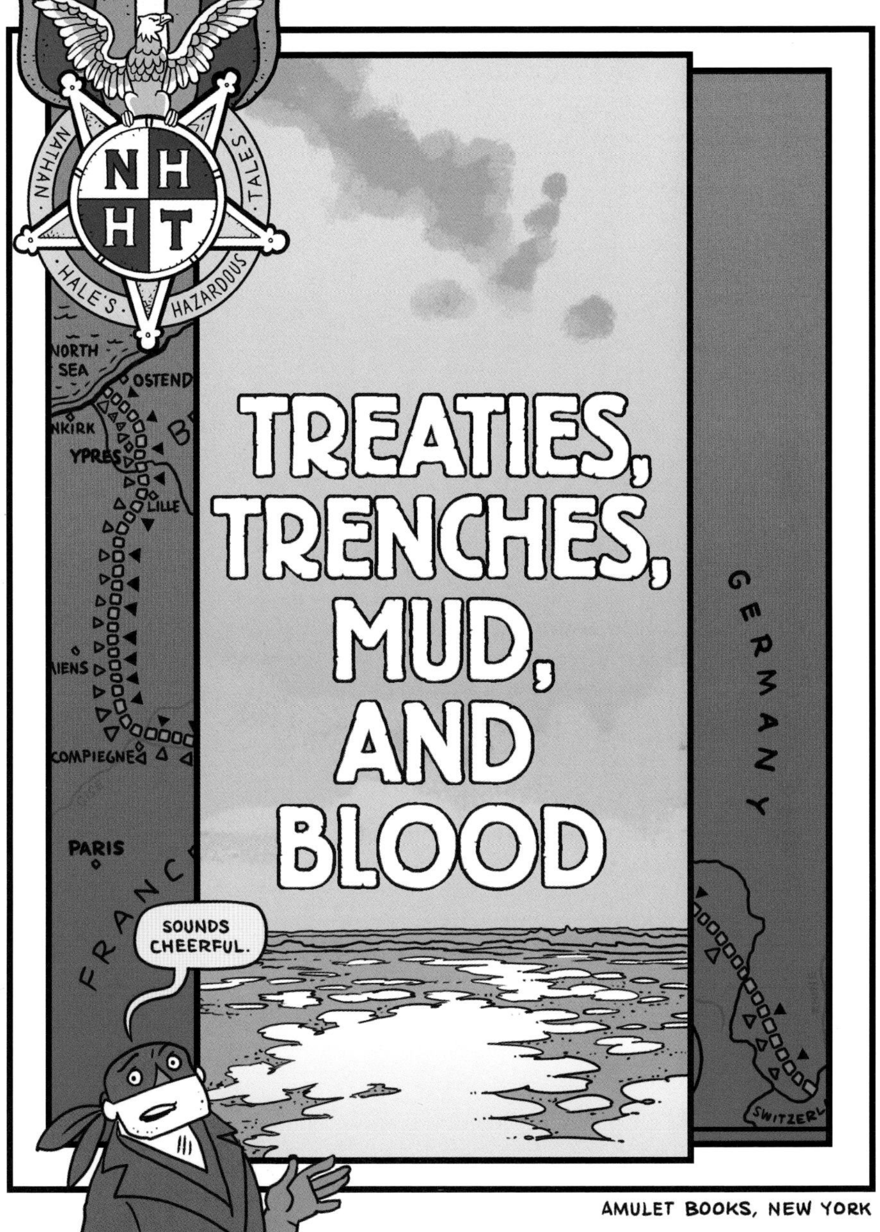

AMULET BOOKS, NEW YORK

LIBRARY OF CONGRESS CONTROL NUMBER: 2013049048
ISBN: 978-1-4197-0808-4

BOOK DESIGN BY NATHAN HALE AND CHAD W. BECKERMAN

PRINTED AND BOUND IN CHINA
19

ABRAMS The Art of Books
195 Broadway, New York, NY 10007
abramsbooks.com

TO MY FIRST WORLD WAR I
TEACHER, SNOOPY

NHHT

THIS PROLOGUE IS BROUGHT TO YOU BY *E PLURIBUS HANGMAN.*
YOUR NAME IS **WHAT?**
HOWE it all started. by HANGMAN
New york 1776
WE WERE GOING TO HANG A SPY NAMED NATHAN HALE.
HIM
(ME, THE HANGMAN)
(CAP'N NATHAN HALE)
(THE PROVOST)
I REGRET THAT I AM A HERO, BLAH BLAH. AMERICA BLAH BLAH. DEATH. AMEN.
CAP'N HALE SAID HIS FAMOUS LAST WORDS
THEN THE GALLOWS TURNED INTO A GIANT BOOK
WHAT'S A GOIN' ON HERE?
RRAAAAAAAWR
YIKES!
THE BOOK ATE THE SPY!
Munch!
(I GOT SCARED.)
DON'T EAT ME!
(IT IS A HISTORY BOOK! REMEMBER THAT.)
HE WENT DOWNE IN HISTORY! THEN THE BOOK SPIT HIM OUT!
I'M BACK AND I KNOW ALL OF HISTORY!
PSHAW!
TELL US A STORY FROM INSIDE THAT BIG HISTORY BOOK!
OR WE WILL HANG YOU!
WE'LL PROB'LY HANG YOU ANYWAY!
HISTORY BOOK
(PROVOST DON'T BELIEVE IT.)
The end.

THANK YOU, HANGMAN. I'M SURE THAT CLEARED UP ANY CONFUSION THE READERS MIGHT HAVE.
I HAVE A GIFT FOR EXPLAINING THINGS. WHAT IS YOUR STORY THIS TIME?

MORE NONSENSE ABOUT AMERICA BEATING ENGLAND, I SUPPOSE?
THERE WILL COME A TIME WHEN AMERICA AND ENGLAND WON'T FIGHT EACH OTHER ANYMORE. IN FACT, THEY BECOME ALLIES AND EVEN BEST FRIENDS!

COUNTRIES CAN HAVE BEST FRIENDS?
INDEED, THEY CAN.

I WANT TO BE BEST FRIENDS WITH TURKEY.
TURKEY?

IT SOUNDS DELICIOUS.

ALLIES IN WHAT SORT OF WAR?
THE GREAT WAR, THE WAR TO END ALL WARS, THEY CALLED IT.
WORLD WAR ONE, TO BE EXACT.

THE WHOLE WORLD FOUGHT EACH OTHER?
PRACTICALLY.

EVEN DELICIOUS TURKEY?
EVEN DELICIOUS TURKEY.

TELL US ABOUT THIS WORLD WAR.
VERY WELL. PREPARE YOURSELVES. WE'RE HEADING TO THE 20TH CENTURY.
IT'S NOT GOING TO BE PRETTY.

I WANT A COMPLETE WAR THIS TIME! BEGINNING-MIDDLE-END--WITH A CLEAR VICTORY AT THE END.
AND IT HAS TO HAVE CRAZY CHARACTERS AND LOTS OF FUNNY JOKES.

THE COMPLETE HISTORY OF WORLD WAR ONE? THAT'S A TALL ORDER.
AND JOKES.

LET ME THINK. IF WE FOCUS ON THE WESTERN FRONT, CUT BACK ON THE EASTERN FRONT AND THE BALKANS, SKIP THE MIDDLE EAST AND LEAVE OUT THE AIR WAR...
HUH?

I THINK WE CAN DO IT! BUT I'M GOING TO HAVE TO TALK FAST--ESPECIALLY IF WE WANT TO GET TO THE PART WHEN THE AMERICANS ARRIVE.
YIPPEE!

TELL ON, PRISONER HALE.

THE YEAR IS 1914. THE AUSTRO-HUNGARIAN EMPIRE, SOMETIMES REFERRED TO AS THE DUAL MONARCHY, OR SIMPLY AUSTRIA-HUNGARY, UNDER THE RULE OF EMPEROR FRANZ JOSEPH, WAS CONCERNED WITH THE GROWING CRISIS IN THE BALKAN PENINSULA. THE INDEPENDENT NATION OF SERBIA, ANGRY OVER THE EMPIRE'S ANNEXATION OF HERZEGOVINA AND BOSNIA IN 1908, WAS BOILING OVER WITH RESENTMENT --AND, SINCE ITS SUCCESSES IN BOTH THE FIRST AND SECOND BALKAN WARS--AMBITION. RUSSIA, SERBIA'S GREAT SLAVIC ALLY, WORRIED AUSTRO- GARIAN EMPIRE EVEN FUR--THER. TENS ACH HIGH WHEN--

HUH?
HUBBA-WHA?

HEY. I DON'T UNDERSTAND ANYTHING YOU'RE SAYING.

I'M FOLLOWING IT QUITE WELL. ONE QUESTION, THOUGH. DOES THE TERM "DUAL MONARCHY" IMPLY TWO MONARCHS OR TWO KINGDOMS UNDER ONE MONARCH?
A FINE QUESTION, PROVOST. TWO COUNTRIES UNDER ONE MONARCH--IN THIS CASE, AUSTRIA AND HUNGARY. THAT MONARCH: EMPEROR FRANZ JOSEPH OF THE HAPSBURG FAMILY. THE HAPSBURG DYNASTY HAD RULED LANDS ALL OVER EUROPE FOR A THOUSAND YEARS.

UGH. CAN YOU TELL A DIFFERENT STORY?
I FIND THIS HIGHLY STIMULATING.

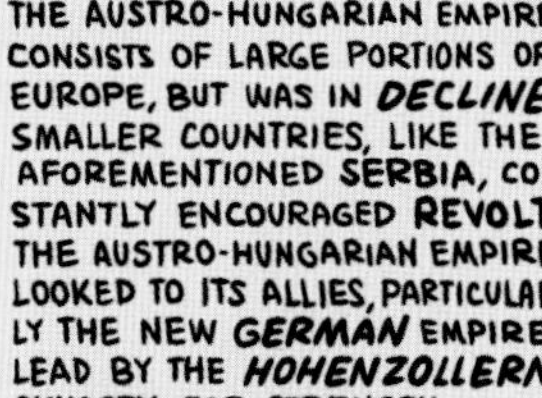
THE AUSTRO-HUNGARIAN EMPIRE CONSISTS OF LARGE PORTIONS OF EUROPE, BUT WAS IN DECLINE. SMALLER COUNTRIES, LIKE THE AFOREMENTIONED SERBIA, CONSTANTLY ENCOURAGED REVOLT. THE AUSTRO-HUNGARIAN EMPIRE LOOKED TO ITS ALLIES, PARTICULARLY THE NEW GERMAN EMPIRE, LEAD BY THE HOHENZOLLERN DYNASTY, FOR STRENGTH--
UGGGHHHHHH! THIS IS SO BORING! WHERE ARE THE JOKES?

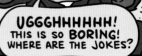

YOU ASKED FOR THIS STORY.
I DIDN'T KNOW IT WOULD BE THIS DULL!

IT ISN'T DULL AT ALL! THIS IS PERFECTLY FASCINATING!
NOT TO ME!

IT'S THE MOST BORING STORY IN THE UNIVERSE!
WHAT WOULD MAKE THIS STORY MORE INTERESTING TO YOU, HANGMAN?

CUTE LITTLE ANIMALS.
OH, FOR CRYING OUT LOUD.

YOU WANT ME TO EXPLAIN WORLD WAR ONE--ONE OF THE WORLD'S MOST DEADLY, HORRIFIC CONFLICTS-- USING CUTE LITTLE ANIMALS?

ALSO, IT WOULD BE NICE IF THEY WORE LITTLE HATS.
YOU HAD TO ASK...

THE READERS OF THIS BOOK WANT CUTE LITTLE HAT-WEARING ANIMALS TOO. DON'T YOU, READERS?

PLEEEEEEE EEEEEEEE EEEEEASE?

OKAY, LET'S DO IT.
HUZZAH!
PLEASE FORGIVE ME, COUNTRIES OF EUROPE AND HISTORIANS EVERYWHERE.
CUE THE CUTE LITTLE ANIMALS.

CHAPTER 1
THE ANCIENT MENAGERIE
HERE IS EUROPE IN 1914. EACH COUNTRY IS NOW REPRESENTED BY AN ANIMAL.
OH JOY! IT'S LIKE A ZOO!
BELGIUM
FRANCE
GERMANY
AUSTRIA
RUSSIA
SERBIA
UNITED KINGDOM
THESE ARE THE KEY PLAYERS IN WORLD WAR ONE. LET'S TAKE A LOOK AT EACH OF THEM.
YEAH! YEAH! YEAH!
LOOK! A MAGIC BIRD AND A PUPPY! THIS IS MY KIND OF STORY!
OOH! WHY ARE THEY SO MAD AT EACH OTHER?
THAT'S AUSTRIA-HUNGARY AND SERBIA--AND THIS IS WHERE WE BEGIN.
THE AUSTRO-HUNGARIAN EMPIRE
REPRESENTED BY: THE GRIFFIN
(SYMBOL OF THE HOUSE OF HAPSBURG)
SERBIA IS A DANGEROUS TROUBLEMAKER! SOMEBODY NEEDS TO TEACH THAT COUNTRY A LESSON!
THE SOONER THE BETTER.
1914 POP. 50 MILLION
LEADER: EMPEROR FRANZ JOSEPH I
ALLIES: GERMANY
THE KINGDOM OF SERBIA
REPRESENTED BY: THE WOLF
(A NATIONAL ANIMAL OF SERBIA)
GIVE ME BACK MY FRIENDS, YOU WICKED OLD BUZZARD!
1914 POP. 4.5 MILLION
LEADER: KING PETER I, P.M. NIKOLA PAŠIĆ
ALLIES: RUSSIA

YOU ANNEXED MY
UDDIES! LET THEM GO!
YEAH!
LET US GO!
BOSNIA
HERZEGOVINA
QUIT YOUR YAPPING, PUPS!
THAT IS NO WAY TO ADDRESS
YOUR EMPEROR!
THIS IS
RIDICULOUS.
BE QUIET--
I FIND THIS 'IGHLY
STIMULATIN'.
WHAT'S THAT? I CAN'T
EAR YOU. MY BEST FRIEND
RUSSIA'S FOOTSTEPS
ARE TOO LOUD!
BOOM
BOOM
SERBIA
YOU WOULDN'T BE SO BRAVE
ON YOUR OWN, PUP!
BOSNIA
HERZEGO
WE HAVE POWERFUL
FRIENDS TOO!
THE RUSSIAN EMPIRE
REPRESENTED BY: THE BEAR
(RUSSIA'S NATIONAL ANIMAL)
RRROARRR!
SERBIA IS UNDER
OUR PROTECTION!
1914 POP. 164 MILLION
LEADER: TSAR
NICHOLAS II
ALLIES: FRANCE, ENGLAND
THE EMPIRE OF GERMANY
REPRESENTED BY: THE EAGLE
(FROM GERMANY'S COAT OF ARMS)
STAY BACK, SERBIA
AND RUSSIA! WE ARE
PREPARED TO FIGHT
FOR OUR ALLY!
1914 POP. 65 MILLION
LEADER: KAISER WILHELM II
ALLIES: AUSTRIA-HUNGARY

RUSSIA COULD STEAMROLL BOTH OF YOU!
THE GERMAN EMPIRE WOULD LIKE TO SEE THEM TRY!
WE ARE PREPARED FOR ANYTHING!
BUT WE ARE BIGGER.
YES, AND SLOWER!
EXCUSEZ-MOI, MESSIEURS, IF YOU MESS WITH RUSSIA, YOU ARE MESSING WITH FRANCE!
YOU!? WE DEFEATED YOU IN 1871!
YOU STOLE OUR LAND! ALSACE-LORRAINE IS OURS! GIVE US THE CHANCE--WE'LL TAKE OUR LANDS AND OUR REVENGE!
RUSSIA
THE REPUBLIC OF FRANCE
REPRESENTED BY: THE GALLIC ROOSTER
DON'T PUSH FRANCE. WE WILL PUSH BACK.
FRANCE
1914 POP. 35 MILLION
LEADER: PRÉSIDENT RAYMOND POINCARÉ
ALLIES: RUSSIA, ENGLAND
THE KINGDOM OF BELGIUM
REPRESENTED BY: THE LION
(BELGIUM'S NATIONAL ANIMAL)
BELGIUM
WHY IS BELGIUM HERE? WE ARE A NEUTRAL COUNTRY! AND WE PLAN TO STAY NEUTRAL!
1914 POP. 7.6 MILLION
LEADER: KING ALBERT I
ALLIES: NEUTRAL

WHY DOES BELGIUM GET TO BE THE LION?
IT'S ENGLAND'S NATIONAL ANIMAL!
THE LION IS A LOT OF COUNTRIES' NATIONAL ANIMAL-- BUT WE CAN'T HAVE TWO LIONS!
ENGLAND WILL BE THE BULLDOG.
THE BULLDOG!? YOU DEVIL!
WHAT'S AMERICA'S ANIMAL?
THE BALD EAGLE, OF COURSE.
OH, NO YOU DON'T! GERMANY IS THE EAGLE!
AMERICA IS THE BALD EAGLE!
IF ENGLAND CAN'T HAVE THE LION, AMERICA CAN'T HAVE THE EAGLE!
MAKE IT A BUNNY!
HA! PERFECT!
VERY WELL.
THE UNITED KINGDOM
REPRESENTED BY: THE BULLDOG
UNITED KINGDOM
1914 POP. 46 MILLION
LEADER: KING GEORGE V
P.M. HERBERT ASQUITH
ALLIES: FRANCE, RUSSIA
THE UNITED STATES OF AMERICA
REPRESENTED BY: THE BALD EAGLE
BUNNY
THIS IS AN OUTRAGE.
AME
AME
1914 POP. 99 MILLION
LEADER: PRESIDENT WOODROW WILSON
ALLIES: NONE (YET)

EVERYONE KEEP CALM! WE HAVE **ALL** SIGNED TREATIES TO KEEP THE PEACE --ESPECIALLY ***YOU,*** GERMANY.
WE HAVE AN ***ALLIANCE,*** FRANCE, ENGLAND, AND RUSSIA, --A ***TRIPLE ENTENTE.***

YEAH. TRIPLE IN A **TENT.**
TRIPLE ENTENTE
FRANCE
RUSSIA
IF YOU ATTACK **ONE** OF US, YOU WILL HAVE TO FIGHT **ALL** OF US.

KEEP YOUR STINKY TENT! WE HAVE A ***TRIPLE ALLIANCE!***
TRIPLE? THERE'S ONLY ***TWO*** OF YOU.

HUH? WHERE DID ***ITALY*** GO?
SOMEONE GO GET THE OTTOMAN EMPIRE --THEY'LL JOIN US.

TRIPLE ENTENTE!
U.K.
FRANCE
GERMANY
RUSSIA
AUSTRIA-HUNGARY
ITALY
?
DUAL ALLIANCE!

ENOUGH OF THIS NONSENSE! EVERYONE GO BACK TO YOUR BUSINESS.
OF COURSE ***YOU*** WANT TO GET BACK TO BUSINESS-- BUSINESS IS ***BOOMING*** FOR BRITAIN.

BUSINESS IS **ALWAYS** BOOMING WHEN YOU'RE THE RICHEST COUNTRY IN THE WORLD.
GERMAN
YOU WON'T BE FOR LONG. SOON OUR NAVY WILL BE STRONGER THAN YOURS-- THEN ***WE'LL*** **OWN THE SEAS!**

WHY YOU--!
WE HAVE TERRITORIES ALL OVER THE **WORLD!** *CANADA, AUSTRALIA, NEW ZEALAND*-- THE SUN NEVER SETS ON THE BRITISH EMPIRE! YOU WOULD BE A **FOOL TO ANGER US!**

NOW WHO NEEDS TO **CALM DOWN?**

NOW I'M CONFUSED! WHAT'S GOING ON? IS THIS THE WAR?
NO, NO, THIS IS JUST A LITTLE BACKGROUND ON THE COUNTRIES. WE'LL GET TO THE WAR SOON ENOUGH.
I BET RUSSIA WINS, THEY'RE THE BIGGEST!
NOT A CHANCE! ENGLAND WILL WIN! WE ARE THE RICHEST AND WE RULE THE SEA!
EACH COUNTRY HAS ITS OWN WAR DEPARTMENT. DAY AND NIGHT, THEY PREPARE FOR THE POSSIBILITY OF WAR.
LET'S SEE WHO IS PLANNING WHAT.
IF WAR STARTS, WE SHALL ATTACK RUSSIA AND FRANCE AT THE SAME TIME!
THE SCHLIEFFEN PLAN
QUICK AND DECISIVE!
US
RUSSIA
FRANCE
GERMAN ARMY SIZE: 750,000
ARMY RESERVE SIZE: 1.5 MILLION
FASTER MOBILIZATION IS KEY TO RUSSIAN VICTORY!
PLAN 19
WE NEED MORE TRAINS!
RUSSIAN ARMY SIZE: 1.4 MILLION
ARMY RESERVE SIZE: 1.7 MILLION
WHAT COLOR PANTALOONS WILL OUR SOLDIERS WEAR?
TRADITIONAL RED, OF COURSE!
PLAN XVII
FRENCH ARMY SIZE: 800,000
ARMY RESERVE SIZE: 2.9 MILLION
WE'VE GOT TO STOMP SERBIA!
ENEMY #1
STOMP SERBIA!
AUSTRO-HUNGARIAN ARMY: 450,000
ARMY RESERVE SIZE: 1.4 MILLION
OUR NAVY MUST REMAIN THE STRONGEST!
PLAN 'W'
INDEED.
UNITED KINGDOM ARMY: 700,000
ARMY RESERVE SIZE: 400,000
WE DON'T HAVE A VERY BIG ARMY-- ARE YOU SURE WE WANT TO TANGLE WITH THESE COUNTRIES?
ABSOLUTELY.
SERBIAN ARMY SIZE: 90,000
ARMY RESERVE SIZE: 420,000

WHAT ARE BELGIUM'S PLANS? YOU DIDN'T SHOW THEM.

YEAH! AND YOU FORGOT AMERICA TOO. I WANNA SEE THOSE BUNNIES!

BELGIUM IS NEUTRAL. THEIR PLAN IS TO STAY OUT OF WAR.

AND YET THEY GET TO BE THE *LIONS*...

AMERICA IS FAR FROM EUROPE, THEY HAVE NO REASON TO GET INVOLVED.

WONDER WHAT THEM COUNTRIES OVERSEAS IS UP TO.

DON'T RIGHTLY KNOW, DON'T RIGHTLY **CARE**.

NONE OF THIS IS ANYTHING NEW --EUROPE HAS ALWAYS BEEN AT WAR WITH ITSELF.

TRUE, BUT WEAPONS ARE BIGGER AND BADDER IN 1914. NEW TECHNOLOGY WILL LEAD TO A WHOLE NEW TYPE OF WAR.

WON'T THEY USE LANCES, GUNS, AND BAYONETS, LIKE ALWAYS?

THEY'LL USE ALL OF THOSE, SURE. BUT THE GUNS ARE BIGGER NOW.

1776 6-POUND HOWITZER

1914 14CM RAIL GUN

WE HAVE ALSO ENTERED THE AGE OF THE *MACHINE GUN*.

WHAT'S A MACHINE GUN? IT LOOKS UGLY.

YOU'LL FIND OUT. AND IT *IS* UGLY.

IF YOUR NEIGHBOR IS STOCKPILING WEAPONS, WHAT DO YOU DO?
MOVE?
YOU BUILD AN ARSENAL YOURSELF!

THIS IS WHAT HAPPENS IN EUROPE. NO COUNTRY *WANTS* WAR--
I THINK GERMANY MIGHT WANT IT.
--BUT EACH COUNTRY *PREPARES* FOR IT.

SENSIBLE. BETTER SAFE THAN SORRY.
BEFORE LONG, EVERYONE WILL BE **SORRY** AND NO ONE WILL BE **SAFE**.

CHAPTER
2
THE BLACK HAND
MOVING AWAY FROM THE ANIMAL METAPHORS--
NO WAY! THE ANIMALS STAY!
THE ANIMALS WERE JUST A WAY TO DIFFERENTIATE COUNTRIES-- THIS IS A TRUE STORY, INVOLVING REAL HUMANS!
YOU'RE JUST MAD ABOUT THE BUNNIES.
FINE! WE'LL KEEP THE ANIMALS! BUT REMEMBER, THIS REALLY HAPPENED-- IT'S NOT SOME ANIMAL FAIRY TALE!
THIS CHAPTER IS ABOUT A YOUNG MAN NAMED GAVRILO PRINCIP. HE GREW UP IN BOSNIA--
SERB UNIT
THAT'S UNDER AUSTRO-HUNGARIAN CONTROL!
HE WANTED HIS COUNTRY TO BE UNIFIED WITH SERBIA.
UNIFICATION OR DEATH!
THESE STUDENT PROTESTS ARE SILLY. IF YOU REALLY WANT UNITY, YOU SHOULD JOIN OUR SECRET FORCE.
SECRET FORCE, WHAT'S IT CALLED?
IT'S CALLED "UNIFICATION OR DEATH."
UNIFICATION OR DEATH!
STUDENTS FOR UNITY!
THAT'S PERFECT!
SSSHHH! OUR CODE NAME IS "THE BLACK HAND."
WOW! WHERE DO I SIGN UP?
SSSSHHH! OVER THERE.
I WISH TO JOIN THE BLACK HAND!
RECRU
YOU?
THE BLACK HAND NEEDS MEN-- NOT SCRAWNY PIPSQUEAKS LIKE YOU. GET LOST, BOY!
HIT THE ROAD, WEAKLING! HA-HA-HA!
WEAKLING!
I'LL SHOW YOU WHAT I CAN DO.

GAVRILO PRINCIP MOVED TO SERBIA.
UNIFICATION OR DEATH!
UNITE!

ALL THIS SHOUTING-- *IT'S JUST **TALK!*** WE SHOULD ***DO*** SOMETHING!
LIKE WHAT?

WE SHOULD ***SHOOT*** AN AUSTRIAN!
ASSASSINATION?
WHO, THE GOVERNOR?

NO. SOMEONE BIGGER, I THINK.
ARCHDUKE FRANZ FERDINAND TO VISIT SARAJEVO IN JUNE
THE **ARCHDUKE**!? **ARE YOU CRAZY**!? HE'S THE NEXT ***EMPEROR*** OF AUSTRIA-HUNGARY!

IF WE DID THIS, THEY'D HAVE TO LET US JOIN THE BLACK HAND!

WE SHOULD ASK THE BLACK HAND FIRST.
FINE.

THE ARCHDUKE!? ARE YOU CRAZY?!
THE ARCHDUKE WILL BE VISITING THE BOSNIAN CITY OF **SARAJEVO**. WE CAN DO THIS--WE ***WILL*** DO THIS.

THIS IS A VERY SERIOUS PROPOSITION. LET ME TALK TO MY SUPERIORS.

THE ARCHDUKE!? ARE THEY CRAZY!?
YES, SIR. I THINK THEY ***ARE*** CRAZY. THEY SEEM TO THINK THEY WILL SUCCEED.

VERY WELL. ARM THEM. TRAIN THEM. LET THEM CARRY OUT THIS MISSION.
IT'S DRASTIC, BUT ANYTHING THAT **HURTS** AUSTRIA-HUNGARY ***HELPS*** OUR CAUSE FOR SERBIA.

YOU ***MUST*** COVER YOUR TRACKS! LEAVE NO EVIDENCE THAT WE ARE CONNECTED WITH THEM.
SERBIAN MILITARY INTELLIGENCE, KALEMEGDAN FORTRESS, BELGRADE

IF ANYONE DISCOVERS THAT SERBIAN MILITARY INTELLIGENCE TRAINED AND ARMED THESE BOYS... THERE COULD BE TROUBLE.

BIG TROUBLE.

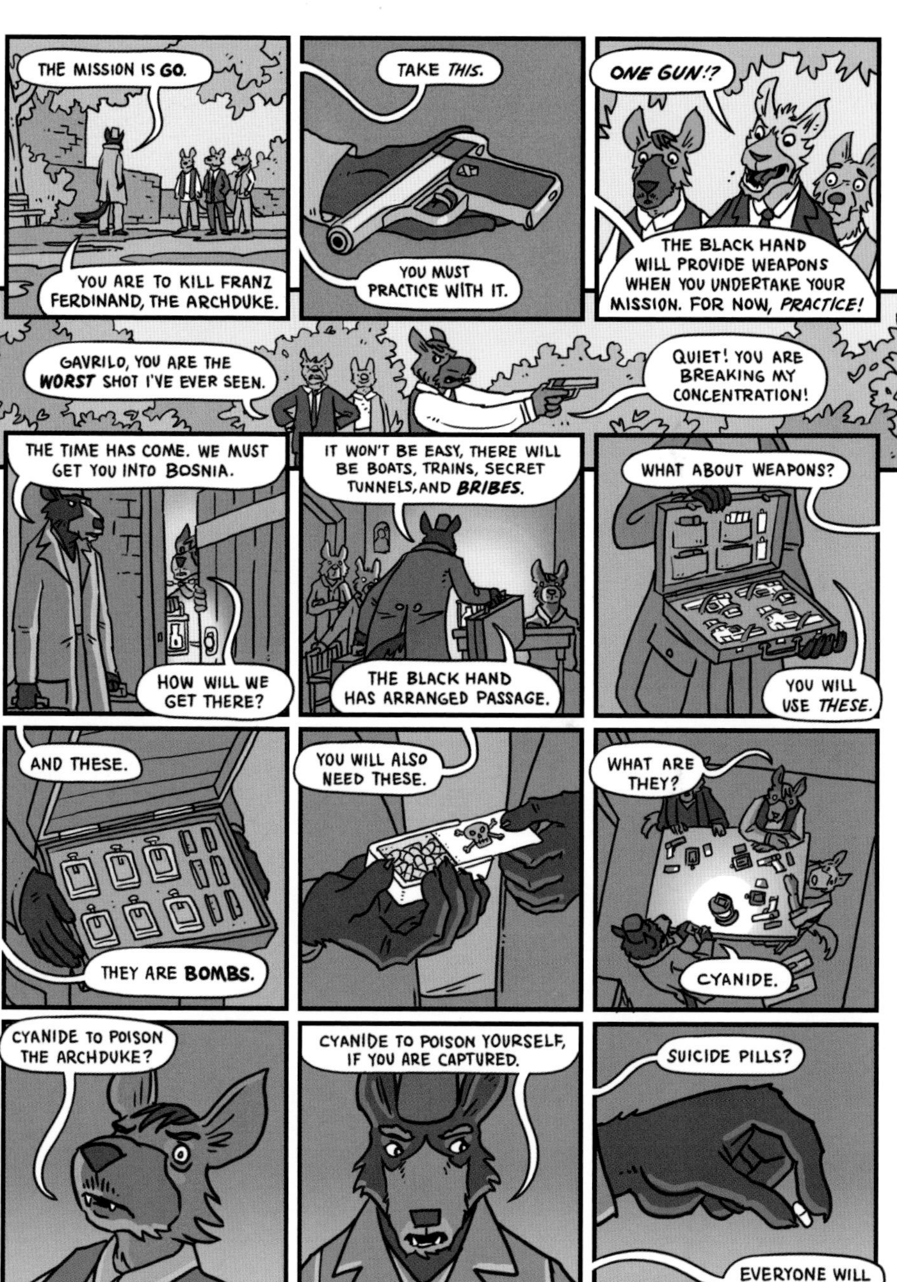
THE MISSION IS GO.
YOU ARE TO KILL FRANZ FERDINAND, THE ARCHDUKE.
TAKE THIS.
YOU MUST PRACTICE WITH IT.
ONE GUN!?
THE BLACK HAND WILL PROVIDE WEAPONS WHEN YOU UNDERTAKE YOUR MISSION. FOR NOW, PRACTICE!
GAVRILO, YOU ARE THE WORST SHOT I'VE EVER SEEN.
QUIET! YOU ARE BREAKING MY CONCENTRATION!
THE TIME HAS COME. WE MUST GET YOU INTO BOSNIA.
HOW WILL WE GET THERE?
IT WON'T BE EASY, THERE WILL BE BOATS, TRAINS, SECRET TUNNELS, AND BRIBES.
THE BLACK HAND HAS ARRANGED PASSAGE.
WHAT ABOUT WEAPONS?
YOU WILL USE THESE.
AND THESE.
THEY ARE BOMBS.
YOU WILL ALSO NEED THESE.
WHAT ARE THEY?
CYANIDE.
CYANIDE TO POISON THE ARCHDUKE?
CYANIDE TO POISON YOURSELF, IF YOU ARE CAPTURED.
SUICIDE PILLS?
EVERYONE WILL CARRY ONE.

DON'T DO THIS, GAVRILO PRINCIP!
THIS REALLY SEEMS LIKE A HORRIBLE SCHEME.

DON'T DO THIS, YOUR EXCELLENCE!
VISITING SARAJEVO ON JUNE 28 IS A BAD IDEA.

WHY IS THAT?
IT'S VIDOVDAN--ST. VITUS DAY, A SERBIAN HOLIDAY. THE NATIONALISTS WILL BE OUT!

I AM THE EMPEROR-TO-BE. I CAN'T LIVE IN FEAR OF SERBIANS. AND SOPHIE WILL BE WITH ME. NOBODY WOULD ATTACK SOPHIE.
THE TOUR WILL CONTINUE AS PLANNED.

YOU THREE WON'T ACT ALONE. THE BLACK HAND HAS TRAINED THESE MEN AS WELL.
YOU MUST SHARE THE WEAPONS.

HEY, IT'S STICKY!
THEY'RE ALL STICKY--THEY WERE SMUGGLED IN A BOX OF SUGAR.

HEY! WHY DON'T I GET A GUN? I'M A MUCH BETTER SHOT THAN GAVRILO!
YOU'LL HAVE A BOMB!

THE BOMBS ARE KEY TO THIS MISSION. YOUR JOB IS TO GET ONE BOMB INTO THE ARCHDUKE'S CAR.
THEN, BOOM!

WE FIGHT FOR THE FREEDOM OF SERBIANS EVERYWHERE. TOMORROW, WE STRIKE A BLOW AGAINST TYRANNY.
I STILL WISH I HAD A GUN.

WHAT A BEAUTIFUL DAY!
YOUR HIGHNESS, IT WOULD BE MUCH SAFER TO PUT THE TOP UP.
ON A BEAUTIFUL DAY LIKE THIS? CERTAINLY NOT! KEEP THE CAR'S TOP *DOWN*.
THERE ARE SEVEN CARS. WHICH CAR? I DON'T KNOW WHICH CAR. *WHICH CAR?*
ASSASSIN #1
JUST THROW THE BOMB. DO IT. THROW THE BOMB. THROW IT. **THROW IT. *THROW IT!*** DON'T THROW IT.
ASSASSIN #2
FOOLS, LOST THEIR NERVE --*BUT I WON'T!*
ASSASSIN #3
TINK
TINK
BOP
BOOM
UNITY OR DEATH!
THE THIRD ASSASSIN, NAMED NEDELJKO ČABRINOVIĆ, WAS PULLED FROM THE RIVER AND BEATEN BY THE CROWD.
THE CYANIDE PILL WAS LONG EXPIRED. INSTEAD OF DYING, HE JUST VOMITED A *LOT*.

I CAN'T SEE! WAS THAT THE ARCHDUKE'S CAR?
NO, NEDELJKO MISSED! IT BLEW UP IN THE STREET!
RETREAT INTO THE CROWD! THE MISSION HAS FAILED.

DRIVE! GET THE ARCHDUKE TO SAFETY!

I CAME HERE ON A VISIT AND I GET BOMBS THROWN AT ME! IT'S OUTRAGEOUS!
I AM SORRY FOR THE OUTBURST. I SHALL GO TO THE HOSPITAL TO VISIT THOSE INJURED IN THE BLAST.

A FINE IDEA.
BUT, YOUR GRACE, THERE COULD BE MORE ASSASSINS OUT THERE.

NONSENSE! WE WILL GO TO THE HOSPITAL.

IF WE STAY OFF OF THE MAIN ROUTES AND DRIVE FAST, WE SHOULD BE SAFE.

WE SHOULD CLOSE THE TOP TOO.
THE TOP STAYS OPEN.

YOU LOOK TERRIBLE. WERE YOU IN THE BOMBING?
ME?

NO! I WASN'T ANYWHERE NEAR THE BOMBING!
WHAT BOMBING?

WHAT CAN I BRING YOU?
HUH?
THIS IS A CAFÉ, YOU ORDER FOOD HERE.

UM, COFFEE AND A BUREK.
WHAT'S A BUREK, SOME KINDA SANDWICH?
MORE LIKE A PIE, BUT CLOSE ENOUGH.

LOOK, THE PEOPLE ARE CHEERING!
THEY SEE THAT WE AREN'T AFRAID OF TERRORISTS.

SORRY, YOUR HIGHNESS, WRONG TURN.
REVERSE, YOU FOOL! THIS ISN'T THE WAY!

BLAST! THE ENGINE IS STALLED.
-GRR-RR
GRR-RR-R
ONE MOMENT, YOUR GRACE.

HUH?
GR-RRR
-RR-RRRG
GR-RRR
BANG
BANG

CHAPTER
3
THE ULTIMATUM
YOU SHOULDN'T HAVE DONE THAT, GAVRILO PRINCIP.

THE ARCHDUKE AND HIS WIFE HAVE BEEN MURDERED!
AUS
ROYAL MURDERS! IT WILL BE WAR!

ONE ASSASSINATION, ESPECIALLY IN THE BALKANS, IS NO CAUSE FOR WAR!
UNI
AUST
SERBIA MUST PAY!

NOT SO FAST.
RUSSIA
GER
YOU CAN COUNT ON OUR FAITHFUL SUPPORT, AUSTRIA-HUNGARY.

CALM DOWN! THERE IS A DIPLOMATIC WAY TO SOLVE THIS!
UNITED KINGD
AUSTRIA-H
WE HAVE SENT SERBIA A NOTE.

A NOTE!? THIS ISN'T A NOTE-- IT'S AN INSANE ULTIMATUM!
SERBIA

THEY WANT US TO SUPPRESS OUR PRESS, DISSOLVE THE BLACK HAND, STOP ALL ANTI-AUSTRO-HUNGARIAN TALK, ALLOW THEIR POLICE TO OPERATE IN SERBIA --AND MORE! THE LIST GOES ON AND ON!
THE ROYAL SERBIAN GOV- -ERNMENT SHALL UNDERTAKE:
AND HERE'S THE BEST PART: "RESPOND WITHIN 48 HOURS, OR WE DECLARE WAR!"

JUST ACCEPT IT! WE'LL SORT IT ALL OUT LATER.
ACCEPT IT? BUT--

DO IT! NONE OF US WANT WAR!

FINE. WE AGREE TO ALL DEMANDS--EXCEPT FOR #6! AUSTRO-HUNGARIAN POLICE CANNOT OPERATE IN SERBIA --THAT'S CRAZY!

SO YOU DON'T ACCEPT THE TERMS OF OUR NOTE?
WE ACCEPT **MOST** OF THEM!
AUS
EUROPE IS TREMBLING ON THE VERGE OF GENERAL ***WAR***!
RUSS
EXTEND IT! EXTEND THE DEADLINE!
NO, I DON'T THINK WE'LL BE EXTENDING ANY DEADLINES, THANK YOU.
YOU ARE SETTING FIRE TO EUROPE!
TIME'S UP.
SERBIA, WE DECLARE WAR.
WHAT!? WHAT'S GOING ON?
THE AUSTRO-HUNGARIANS JUST DECLARED WAR ON SERBIA!
THE ***FOOLS***!
TO MY COUSIN, KAISER WILHELM,
AN IGNOBLE WAR HAS BEEN DECLARED ON A WEAK COUNTRY. IN THE NAME OF OUR OLD FRIENDSHIP, DO WHAT YOU CAN TO STOP YOUR ALLIES FROM GOING TOO FAR.
-Nicky
TSAR NICHOLAS OF RUSSIA
I AM EXERTING MY UTMOST INFLUENCE TO INDUCE THE AUSTRIANS TO ARRIVE AT A SATISFACTORY UNDERSTANDING WITH YOU.
YOUR FRIEND AND COUSIN,
Willy
KAISER WILHELM OF GERMANY
THAT'S BETTER. SEE, EVEN THE LEADERS OF GERMANY AND RUSSIA AGREE--WE SHOULD ***ALL*** CALM DOWN.
NICE TRY, BULLDOG. BUT I DON'T THINK ANYONE IS CALMING DOWN.

CHAPTER 4
MOBILIZATION
"MOBOZILLATION"? WHAT DOES THAT MEAN?
IT MEANS ASSEMBLING YOUR FORCES, DISTRIBUTING WEAPONS AND SUPPLIES--IT MEANS YOU PLAN TO FIGHT.
MOBILIZING IS LIKE DRAWING YOUR SWORD.
SERBIA, PREPARE TO DIE.
WE ARE MOBILIZING AS FAST AS WE CAN!
UM, RUSSIA? ARE YOU GOING TO HELP?
HUNGARY
SERBIA
I'M CONFUSED. WORLD WAR ONE WAS FOUGHT WITH MEDIEVAL WEAPONS?
NO, NO, THIS IS JUST A VISUAL METAPHOR FOR WAR PREPARATION.
DON'T WORRY, WE'LL SEE PLENTY OF 20TH CENTURY WARFARE SOON ENOUGH.
TROOPS ARE ASSEMBLED AND MOVED TO THE BORDERS.
FRANCE AND GERMANY HAVE TRAINS IN PLACE. THEY MOBILIZE QUICKLY.
RUSSIA HAS FEW TRAINS, THEY MOBILIZE SLOWLY.

EVERYBODY STOP MOBILIZING!
UNITED KINGD
IF WE ARE FAST ENOUGH, WE CAN DEFEAT FRANCE BEFORE RUSSIA'S EVEN READY.
IF YOU THINK WE'LL BE EASY TO DEFEAT, YOU ARE DEAD WRONG.
I GET IT. NOBODY WANTS TO BE THE ONE CAUGHT WITH THEIR PANTS DOWN.
SO TO SPEAK.
SIX MILLION SOLDIERS MOBILIZE ACROSS EUROPE.
IT TAKES ARMIES TO FEED THESE ARMIES. MILES AND MILES OF SUPPLY LINES STRETCH ACROSS EUROPE; WEAPONS, AMMUNITION, AND FOOD MUST BE PROVIDED.
THE ROADS FILL WITH SOLDIERS, VEHICLES AND HORSES.
WHICH COUNTRY DO THE HORSES REPRESENT?
THE HORSES REPRESENT HORSES.

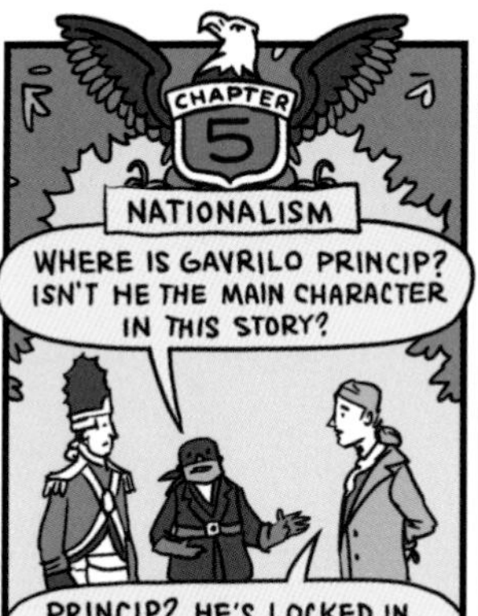
CHAPTER
5
NATIONALISM
WHERE IS GAVRILO PRINCIP? ISN'T HE THE MAIN CHARACTER IN THIS STORY?
PRINCIP? HE'S LOCKED IN A SERBIAN JAIL, WHERE HE'LL SPEND THE REST OF THE WAR.

THEN WHO IS THE MAIN CHARACTER OF THIS TALE?
THIS STORY IS SO LARGE AND COMPLICATED--IT'S BEST TO THINK OF THE COUNTRIES AS THE MAIN CHARACTERS.

OH. THEN WHO ARE THE GOOD GUYS?

WE ARE!
AUSTRIA
WE ARE PRESERVING OUR ANCIENT EMPIRE FROM THE SERBIANS. THEY KILLED THE HEIR TO OUR THRONE!

WE ARE!
SER
WE ARE FIGHTING AN OPPRESSIVE TYRANT! UNIFICATION OR DEATH!

WE ARE!
SERBIA IS UNDER RUSSIA'S PROTECTION!

WE ARE!

WE ARE LOYAL TO OUR ALLY AUSTRIA-HUNGARY!

WE ARE!
WE WILL NOT ALLOW ANYONE TO INVADE FRANCE!

WE ARE!
LAWS AND TREATIES MUST BE UPHELD! WE CAN'T LET COUNTRIES INVADE OTHER COUNTRIES WILLY-NILLY!

SO WHO ARE THE *BAD GUYS?*
THEY ARE!

THIS, *RIGHT HERE,* IS ONE OF THE MAIN CAUSES OF WORLD WAR ONE-- NATIONALISM.
GERMANY IS THE BEST! EAGLES RULE!
YOU ARE ALL STUPID! VIVE LA FRANCE!
BOW DOWN! THE EMPIRE OF AUSTRIA-HUNGARY IS *SUPERIOR!*
DOWN WITH GRIFFINS! UP WITH WOLVES!

LOOKS LIKE OLD-FASHIONED *PATRIOTISM* TO ME.

PATRIOTISM IS WHEN YOU LOVE YOUR COUNTRY. ***NATIONALISM*** IS WHEN YOU LOVE YOUR COUNTRY AND ***HATE*** ALL OTHER COUNTRIES.

ENOUGH OF THIS METAPHORICAL **MISHMASH**! LET'S GET INTO THE TACTICS AND MANEUVERS-- THE ADVANCES AND RETREATS!
THE SHOOTY-SHOOTY **BANG-BANG!**

ALLOW ME ONE MORE BIG METAPHORICAL SCENE,
THEN WE'LL GET TO THE SHOOTY-SHOOTY BANG-BANG.

HERE WE SEE THE **CAUSES** OF **WORLD WAR ONE.** EUROPE BUILT A RAMP OUT OF DANGEROUS ***"ISMS"***-- NATIONALISM, MILITARISM, AND IMPERIALISM. THE ASSASSINATION OF ARCHDUKE FRANZ FERDINAND CAUSED EVERYONE AND THEIR ALLIES TO MOBILIZE AND CHARGE INTO ***WAR.***

WHO'S THAT BEEFY FELLOW WITH THE STEW POT?

THAT'S ***ARES,*** THE GREEK **GOD OF WAR,** OBVIOUSLY.

RUSSIA

AUSTRIA HUNGARY

UNITED KINGDOM

NATIONALISM

GERMANY

ALLIANCES

IMPERIALISM

1914
CHARGE!
FRANCE
MILITARISM
ASSASSINATION
BANG
HOLY MACKEREL! GREEK GODS, WEIRD STATUES, ANIMALS IN ARMOR--THIS SCENE IS COMPLETELY BATTY!
THE CAUSES OF WORLD WAR ONE ARE COMPLICATED.
BATTY, INDEED. LET'S GET ON TO THAT SHOOTY-BANG.

CHAPTER 6
THE KING OF THE BELGIANS

ROYAL PALACE
BRUSSELS, BELGIUM

EVERYONE IS DECLARING WAR ON EACH OTHER. IT MAKES ME PROUD TO BE BELGIAN AND NEUTRAL.

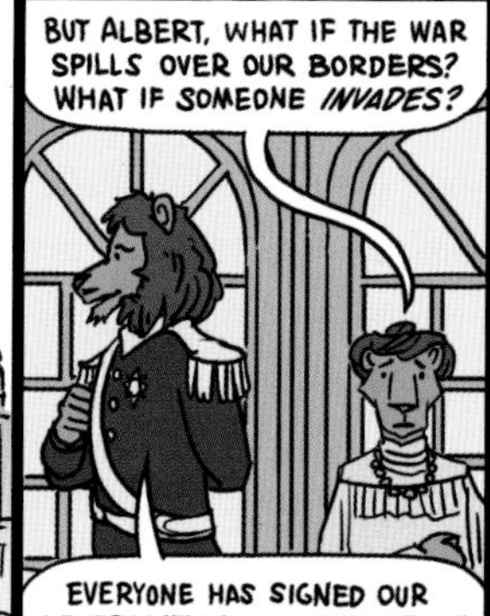

BUT ALBERT, WHAT IF THE WAR SPILLS OVER OUR BORDERS? WHAT IF SOMEONE *INVADES?*
EVERYONE HAS SIGNED OUR NEUTRALITY AGREEMENT, THEY AREN'T *ALLOWED* TO INVADE.

KING ALBERT, YOUR MAJESTY, A MESSAGE FROM **GERMANY**:

AUGUST 2, 1914
TO THE BELGIAN MINISTER
OF FOREIGN AFFAIRS,

WE HAVE RELIABLE INFORMATION THAT **FRANCE** IS PLANNING TO MARCH THROUGH BELGIUM IN ORDER TO INVADE GERMANY.

WE FEAR THAT BELGIUM WILL NOT BE ABLE TO REPEL A LARGE FRENCH INVASION FORCE.

THEREFORE, FOR YOUR PROTECTION AND OURS, WE REQUIRE YOUR PERMISSION TO ENTER BELGIUM.

THE SNEAKY DEVILS! THEY WANT TO SAVE US FROM ***INVASION*** BY ***INVADING US!***
FRANCE IS OUR FRIEND, THEY WOULD *NEVER* INVADE US!

DOES GERMANY THINK WE'LL BELIEVE THIS? HOW STUPID DO THEY THINK WE ARE?
THEY PLAN TO INVADE FRANCE --AND I SUSPECT THEY WANT TO USE *US* AS THEIR INVASION ROUTE.

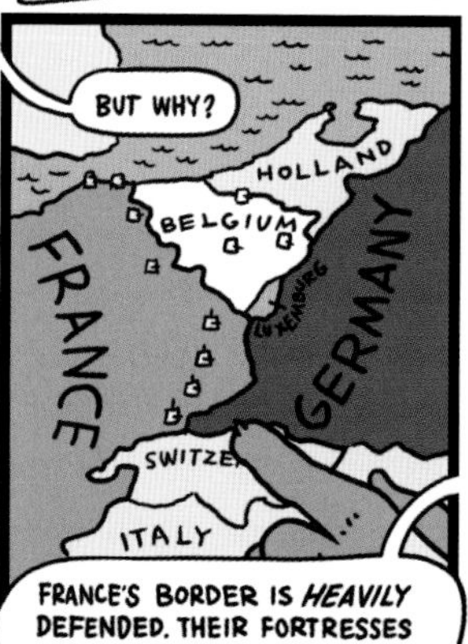

BUT WHY?
HOLLAND
BELGIUM
FRANCE
GERMANY
SWITZE
ITALY
FRANCE'S BORDER IS *HEAVILY* DEFENDED. THEIR FORTRESSES FORM A STRONG BARRIER.

WE HAVE STRONG FORTRESSES TOO!
THAT'S WHY THE GERMANS ARE ASKING *NICELY.*

IF WE LET THEM MARCH THROUGH OUR BORDERS THEY WILL BYPASS *ALL* OF FRANCE'S DEFENSES.
WE'RE A *NATION*-- NOT A *ROAD!*

THERE'S MORE:
"IF BELGIUM OPPOSES OUR PASSAGE, SHE WILL BE CONSIDERED AN *ENEMY*."
THEY'VE GIVEN US TWELVE HOURS TO REPLY.

OUR *ENTIRE* ARMY IS **SEVEN** DIVISIONS. THE GERMANS ARE SENDING *THIRTY-FOUR!*
DO WE HAVE ANY HEAVY ARTILLERY?

WE ARE AWAITING A LARGE ORDER OF HEAVY ARTILLERY PIECES FROM THE *KRUPP* STEEL FACTORY--
KRUPP
105MM
THE *KRUPP* STEEL FACTORY IN *GERMANY?* I DON'T THINK WE'LL BE GETTING THAT ORDER.

IF WE ARE TO BE CRUSHED, LET US BE CRUSHED GLORIOUSLY.
WHAT CHOICE DO WE HAVE? WE CAN'T ALLOW THEM PASSAGE!

OUR ANSWER MUST BE *"NO,"* WHATEVER THE CONSEQUENCES.

KING ALBERT OF BELGIUM

UNBELIEVABLE. THE BELGIANS ARE GOING TO *RESIST*.
ARE THEY *INSANE?*

IF WE DON'T DEFEAT FRANCE **QUICKLY**, WE'LL HAVE **RUSSIA** AT OUR BACKS. WE'LL BE CAUGHT BETWEEN *HAMMER AND ANVIL!*
OUR PASSAGE THROUGH BELGIUM IS A MATTER OF *LIFE OR DEATH* FOR GERMANY.

SORRY, BELGIUM, YOU ARE NOW AT WAR WITH GERMANY.
BELGIUM DOESN'T MAKE *WAR*, THEY MAKE *CHOCOLATE!*

DO THEY EVEN *HAVE* AN ARMY?
MAYBE THEIR ARMY IS MADE OF **CHOCOLATE**! HA-HA

BELGIUM HAS GUARANTEED NEUTRALITY--AND WE'RE *BREAKING IT!*
ENGLAND WILL ATTACK US FOR THIS.
ENGLAND WILL ATTACK US ANYWAY.

FORWARD! THERE ISN'T A MINUTE TO LOSE!
I HAVE A PRECISE TIMETABLE! ONE MILLION TROOPS, ELEVEN THOUSAND TRAINS--*ALL TIMED* ***PERFECTLY!***

BLOW UP ALL OF OUR BRIDGES ON THE GERMAN BORDER--RAILROADS AND TUNNELS TOO!

SHOULD WE CALL FRANCE OR ENGLAND FOR HELP?
NOT JUST YET.
SURELY THE KAISER WILL COME TO HIS SENSES AND CALL OFF THIS ***MAD*** INVASION.

THE BRIDGE AT VISÉ, DESTROYED AUGUST 4, 1914

I **LIKE** THIS KING ALBERT. HE'S A BRAVE MAN IN A DIFFICULT POSITION.
I STILL THINK ENGLAND SHOULD BE THE LIONS.

BELGIUM **DESERVES** TO BE THE LIONS! THEY ARE ABOUT TO FIGHT THE GERMANS WITH A ***CHOCOLATE ARMY!***
HANGMAN, I HATE TO DISAPPOINT YOU... BUT--

BUT WHAT? AWWWW. THEY AREN'T MADE OF CHOCOLATE, ARE THEY?
I THOUGHT THAT SOUNDED TOO GOOD TO BE TRUE.

CHAPTER
7
THE BULLDOG STEPS IN
THE GERMANS HAVE INVADED BELGIUM!
WE CAN'T ALLOW THEM TO DO THAT!
ISSUE AN ULTIMATUM, "STOP THE INVASION OR ENGLAND WILL DECLARE WAR ON GERMANY!"
IT'S TIME TO SHOW OFF OUR SEA POWER! SEND THE NAVY TO PROTECT FRANCE'S COAST AND BLOCKADE GERMANY!
UNITED KINGDOM
BELGIUM
FRANCE
GERMANY
GOOD LUCK GETTING PAST US, GERMAN SHIPS!
YOU WON'T GET BY BRITAIN'S NORTHERN PATROL!
OR THE DOVER PATROL!
THE MAN IN CHARGE OF BRITAIN'S NAVY IS NAMED WINSTON CHURCHILL.
FIRST LORD OF THE ADMIRALTY
ONE DAY HE WILL BECOME ONE OF ENGLAND'S GREATEST LEADERS. BUT THAT'S ANOTHER STORY.
WHAT ABOUT ENGLAND'S ARMY?
BRITAIN WAS NOT KNOWN FOR HAVING A LARGE ARMY.
ONE GERMAN LEADER JOKED:
IF BRITAIN'S ARMY EVER INVADES GERMANY, I WILL HAVE IT ARRESTED.
CHEEKY!

CHAPTER 8
FORTRESS: LIÈGE
AUGUST 4, 1914
DEUTSCHLAND, DEUTSCHLAND ÜBER ALLES, ÜBER ALLES IN DER WELT, WENN ES STETS ZU SCHUTZ UND TRUTZE BRÜDERLICH ZUSAMMENHÄLT.
A STIRRING HYMN OF BATTLE!
YEAH. NO NATIONALISM HERE.
*GERMANY, GERMANY ABOVE EVERYTHING, ABOVE EVERYTHING IN THE WORLD, WHEN, FOR PROTECTION AND DEFENSE, IT ALWAYS TAKES A BROTHERLY STAND TOGETHER.
HALT!
WHAT IS THIS!? THE BRIDGE HAS BEEN DESTROYED!
WHY WOULD THE BELGIANS DESTROY THEIR OWN BRIDGE?
DON'T WORRY, THIS IS ONLY TOKEN RESISTANCE, THEY WON'T INTERRUPT OUR MARCH--
BANG
--I COULD BE WRONG.
I DON'T UNDERSTAND. THE BELGIANS ARE SHOOTING--
SHOOTING--AT US!
STOP SINGING! START SHOOTING!
PREPARE THE PONTOONS, WE'LL BUILD OUR OWN BRIDGE!
ARTILLERY FORWARD!
I CAN'T BELIEVE THE BELGIANS ARE SHOOTING AT US!
YOU ARE AN INVADING ARMY! OF COURSE THEY ARE SHOOTING!

WHAT'S THE NAME OF THIS CHOCOLATE CITY?
IT'S LIÈGE. THE CITY HAS A FEW STRONG FORTS AROUND IT.

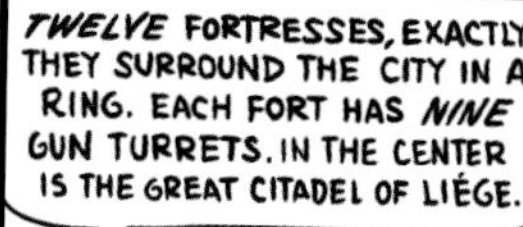
TWELVE FORTRESSES, EXACTLY. THEY SURROUND THE CITY IN A RING. EACH FORT HAS NINE GUN TURRETS. IN THE CENTER IS THE GREAT CITADEL OF LIÉGE.

IT'S A MARVEL, REALLY. I'D SAY IT'S THE SECOND STRONGEST FORTRESS IN ALL OF EUROPE.

HOW DO YOU KNOW ALL OF THAT?
SPIES?
NO. I VACATIONED HERE ONCE.

YOU CAME HERE FOR FUN?
OH, YES. I ENJOY FORTS.

WHO WAS THAT?
THAT WAS MAJOR GENERAL ERICH LUDENDORFF, FROM THE SECOND ARMY.

WHAT'S HE DOING HERE?
MAYBE HE'S STILL ON VACATION.

TRULY A MARVELOUS FORT!
IT'S A SHAME WE'LL HAVE TO OBLITERATE IT.

SIR, THE ATTACK ON FORT DE BARCHON HAS FAILED! WE SUFFERED HEAVY CASUALTIES!
BELGIUM WAS SUPPOSED TO BE EASY!

WE HAVE A FEW TRICKS UP OUR SLEEVE.
SEND IN THE ZEPPELIN.

SHOOT IT DOWN!
Z.V.
SURRENDER, OR WE WILL SEND MORE ZEPPELINS!
YOUR ZEPPELIN KILLED NINE BEFORE OUR ARTILLERY WOUNDED IT. SEND MORE, WE'LL SHOOT THEM ALL DOWN!

THE **CITADEL** IS THE CENTRAL FORT. IF WE CAN CAPTURE IT, THE REST WILL FALL.

PONTISSE
LANTIN
LIERS
LONCIN
LIÈGE
FLÉRON
EMBOURG
CHAUDFONTAI

SEND IN THE "*ENGLISH*" SQUAD.

HELLO! YOU IN THE CITADEL!

LET US IN, WE ARE ENGLISH.

YOU DON'T FOOL US! YOU ARE **GERMANS** IN ***DISGUISE***!

WELL, IT WAS WORTH A TRY.

WHY DIDN'T WE BRING THE ***BIG GUNS***?

THE BIG GUNS ARE EN ROUTE, BUT THEY MOVE **SLOWLY**, THEY ARE **BIG** GUNS.

THEN WHAT DO WE DO? GO UP AND ***KNOCK*** ON THE DOOR?!

WHY NOT?

WHERE IS HE GOING?

HE'S DRIVING UP TO KNOCK ON THE DOOR!

KNOCK
KNOCK
KNOCK

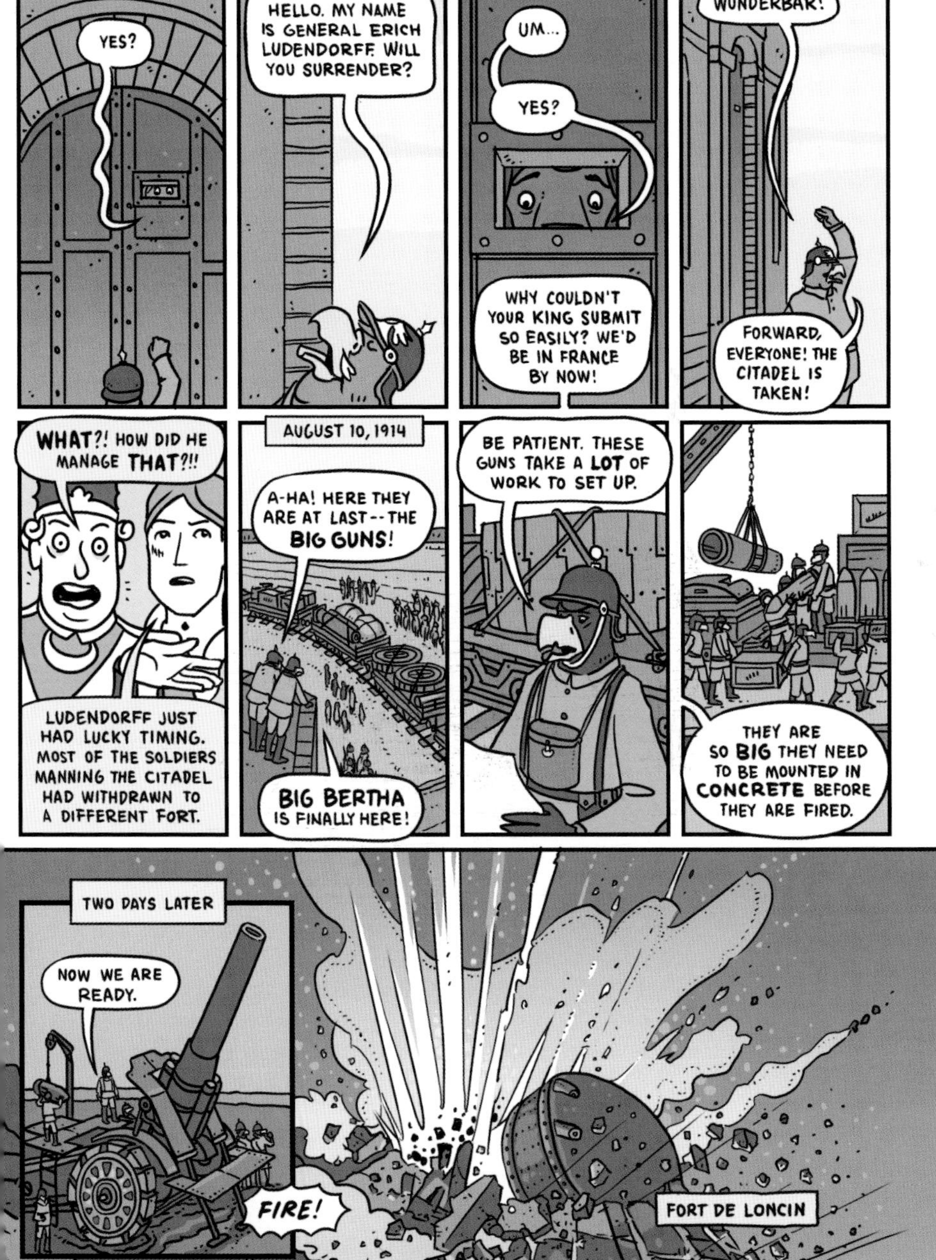
YES?
HELLO. MY NAME IS GENERAL ERICH LUDENDORFF. WILL YOU SURRENDER?
UM...
YES?
WHY COULDN'T YOUR KING SUBMIT SO EASILY? WE'D BE IN FRANCE BY NOW!
WUNDERBAR!
FORWARD, EVERYONE! THE CITADEL IS TAKEN!
WHAT?! HOW DID HE MANAGE THAT?!!
LUDENDORFF JUST HAD LUCKY TIMING. MOST OF THE SOLDIERS MANNING THE CITADEL HAD WITHDRAWN TO A DIFFERENT FORT.
AUGUST 10, 1914
A-HA! HERE THEY ARE AT LAST--THE BIG GUNS!
BIG BERTHA IS FINALLY HERE!
BE PATIENT. THESE GUNS TAKE A LOT OF WORK TO SET UP.
THEY ARE SO BIG THEY NEED TO BE MOUNTED IN CONCRETE BEFORE THEY ARE FIRED.
TWO DAYS LATER
NOW WE ARE READY.
FIRE!
FORT DE LONCIN

CHAPTER 9

THE BATTLE OF CER

WOLVES VS. GRIFFINS
ROUND 1

WHY ARE WE INVADING SERBIA THROUGH THE *MOUNTAINS?*

CER MOUNTAINS, SERBIA
AUGUST 15, 1914

WE SHOULD HAVE INVADED WHERE IT WAS *FLAT!*

THE AUSTRO-HUNGARIANS ARE *TERRIBLE* SOLDIERS!
INEXPERIENCED FOOLS!

WE JUST FOUGHT *TWO* BALKAN WARS-- THESE CLOWNS ARE **CLUELESS**.

RUN, YOU COWARDS!
GO BACK TO AUSTRIA-HUNGARY AND *DON'T COME BACK!*

SERBIA WAS SUPPOSED TO BE AN *EASY TARGET!*
HOW MANY CASUALTIES?

AT LEAST **8,000** OF OUR SOLDIERS ARE DEAD, 50,000 ARE CAPTURED OR WOUNDED.
AAAAAGH!

VICTORY FOR **SERBIA!**

CHAPTER
10
INVISIBLE GUERRILLAS
LOUVAIN, BELGIUM
AUGUST 1914
IF THE BELGIANS HAD JUST *LET US THROUGH* WE WOULDN'T HAVE TO BURN THEIR TOWNS.
YOU BROUGHT THIS ON YOURSELVES!

KEEP YOUR EYES OPEN. THE BELGIAN RESISTANCE HAS **SNIPERS** EVERYWHERE.
GUERRILLA SNIPERS!

HOLD ON! WHICH COUNTRY IS THE **GORILLAS**?
GUERRILLAS --RESISTANCE FIGHTERS.
SOMEONE WHO FIGHTS THEIR COUNTRY'S ENEMIES BEHIND THE FRONT LINES, IN SECRET, WITHOUT UNIFORMS.

LOOK! A HORSE WITHOUT A RIDER!
CLIP CLOP CLATTER
A SNIPER MUST HAVE *KILLED* THE RIDER!

A SNIPER!?
SNIPERS!? WHERE!?
THERE ARE **SNIPERS** IN ALL OF THE BUILDINGS!

WE CAN'T HAVE SNIPERS! ***BURN THE TOWN!***

THE *WHOLE* TOWN?
IT'S SUCH A PRETTY TOWN.
BELGIUM MUST BE TAUGHT A LESSON: ***TOWNS WITH SNIPERS WILL BE BURNED TO THE GROUND!***

PLEASE, SIR, DON'T BURN THE LIBRARY! I BEG YOU.
THERE ARE BOOKS IN HERE FROM THE MIDDLE AGES--PRICE-LESS ANCIENT MANUSCRIPTS!

DON'T BLAME US. BLAME THE SNIPERS.

LET THIS BE A LESSON TO ALL WHO RESIST.
BURN IT TO THE GROUND.

LOOK WHAT GERMANY IS DOING TO A *NEUTRAL* COUNTRY!
LOUVAIN DESTROYED
WE MUST STOP THIS!
SUCH A SHAME! SOMEBODY SHOULD **STOP** THIS!
BELGIUM BURNS
NOT US, BUT *SOMEBODY.*
AUGUST 20, 1914
BRUSSELS, BELGIUM
THEY INVADE OUR COUNTRY, BURN OUR CITIES, AND NOW THEY HAVE A PARADE?

WE HAVE CONQUERED BELGIUM!
THE RUSSIANS HAVE INVADED, YOUR IMPERIAL HIGHNESS. THEY ARE ATTACKING EAST PRUSSIA.

WHAT?! THE BEARS ARE SUPPOSED TO BE **SLOW**!
SOMEHOW THEY HAVE MOBILIZED QUICKLY. WE ARE NOW FIGHTING ON *TWO FRONTS*.

WE'RE COMING FOR YOU, GERMANY.
BERLIN? WHEN WE'RE THROUGH, IT'LL BE CALLED ***BEAR***-LIN!

CHAPTER 11

"ALL THE COURAGE IN THE WORLD CANNOT PREVAIL AGAINST GUNFIRE"

AUGUST 22, 1914
ROSSIGNOL, FRANCE

BRAVE LITTLE BELGIUM HAS SLOWED THE GERMAN ADVANCE--AT GREAT COST. NOW IT'S OUR TURN.

THERE ARE **SEVEN** ARMIES IN THE INVASION FORCE. WE HAVE **SIX**.

I'D FEEL BETTER IF WE HAD ONE MORE ARMY!
WHERE ARE THOSE ENGLISH BULLDOGS?
YES, WHERE *ARE* THEY?

FASTER! FASTER! WE MUST GAIN AS MUCH GROUND AS POSSIBLE!

TO PARIS!

SIR, THE *FRENCH* HAVE BEEN SPOTTED.

DIG IN, PREPARE THE ARTILLERY!

DIG IN? WHAT IF THEY **CHARGE**?

WE *WANT* THEM TO CHARGE.

PREPARE TO CHARGE.

BUT, SIR, THE ARTILLERY--

WE CHARGE! WE DON'T **CRAWL**! WE ARE ROOSTERS, NOT ***WORMS***!

CHARGE!

CHARGE!

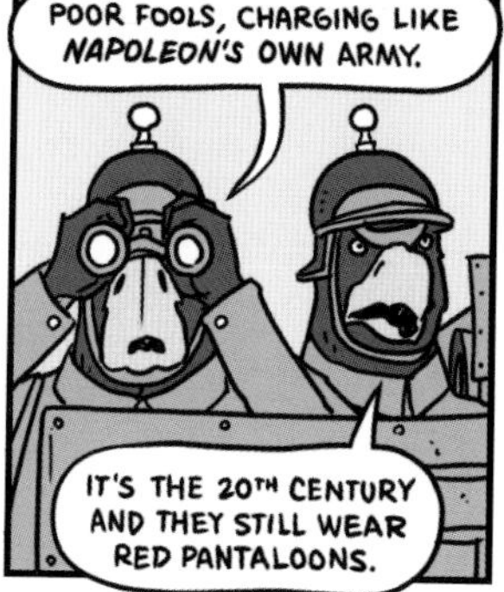

POOR FOOLS, CHARGING LIKE *NAPOLEON'S* OWN ARMY.
IT'S THE 20TH CENTURY AND THEY STILL WEAR RED PANTALOONS.

BRAVE MEN. IT TAKES COURAGE TO CHARGE THE ENEMY HEAD-ON.
THESE TACTICS COST THE FRENCH 200,000 SOLDIERS IN THE FIRST MONTH OF THE WAR.

IF WE CAN'T BEAT THE FRENCH, THE RUSSIANS WILL STEAMROLL US.
SHOW NO MERCY.

CHAPTER 12
THE BATTLE OF MONS
AUGUST 23, 1914 MONS, BELGIUM
GERMAN ADVANCE
CANAL
NIMY
JEMAPPES
MONS
RAIL
TAKE UP POSITIONS ALONG THIS CANAL. WE'LL GIVE THE GERMANS A GOOD SURPRISE!
DO THEY EVEN KNOW WE'RE HERE?
THEY SHOULD, IT WAS IN THE PAPER YESTERDAY.
BRITISH ARRIVE!
HERE THEY COME!
MAKE YOUR SHOTS COUNT! WE'RE OUTNUMBERED THREE TO ONE!
AT·RATATAT·RATATAT·RATATATAT·RATATATATAT·RAT
MAKE WAY! LT. DEASE WAS SHOT FIVE TIMES, BUT KEPT HIS MACHINE GUN FIRING!
WHO'S HOLDING THE SECOND BRIDGE NOW?
PRIVATE GODLEY-- BY HIMSELF!
OY! THERE'S A SWIMMER-- A GERMAN SWIMMER!
DON'T WASTE SHOTS! WHAT CAN ONE SWIMMER DO?
HE'S TURNING THE SWING BRIDGE!
SHOOT HIM! SHOOT HIM! WASTE YOUR BULLETS!
PRIVATE GODLEY! FALL BACK!
RATATATATATAT
I'LL GO LAST! YOU GO! GO!
WHAT'S HE DOING?
HE'S BREAKING DOWN HIS MACHINE GUN--C'MON, GODLEY! NO TIME FOR THAT!
YOU MAY CAPTURE ME, BUT YOU WON'T GET THIS MACHINE GUN!
SPLASH

BLOW THE BRIDGES! WE'RE NEARLY OVERRUN!
THE CHARGES MUST NOT BE CONNECTED.
I'M CAPTAIN WRIGHT, OF THE ROYAL ENGINEERS --I'LL GO PLUG THEM IN!
ARE YOU CRAZY, SIR?
WE CAN'T LET THEM CROSS!
I'LL DO THE OTHER ONE!
KRUMP
GOOD SHOW! HOW'S CAPTAIN WRIGHT DOING?
HE'S WOUNDED, SIR. SHOT.
WHERE IS HE, WITH A MEDIC?
NO, SIR, HE WENT BACK OUT.
MUST BLOW IT UP MUST BLOW IT UP...
CAPTAIN WRIGHT, ARE YOU ALL RIGHT?
I WILL BE, WHEN WE FINALLY BLOW UP THIS BLASTED BRIDGE!

FORGET THE BRIDGES! THE GERMANS ARE BUILDING THEIR OWN PONTOON BRIDGES!

SIR, THE FRENCH FIFTH ARMY IS RETREATING!
KLUCK
BULOW
HAUSEN
B.E.F.
LANREZAC
WHAT!? WE CAN HOLD THIS POSITION!

NOT IF LANREZAC'S FIFTH ARMY ISN'T GUARDING OUR FLANK!
WE'LL BE SITTING DUCKS!

CURSE GENERAL LANREZAC! WE NEED TO RETREAT! PULL BACK!
BUT THE BRIDGE--
LEAVE IT!

WHY ISN'T THE FIFTH ARMY HOLDING THEIR GROUND?
THEY WEREN'T POSITIONED AS WELL AS THE B.E.F.

THE **BEEF**?
THE B.E.F., IT STANDS FOR BRITISH EXPEDITIONARY FORCE.
1,600 B.E.F. SOLDIERS DIED AT MONS. OVER 5,000 GERMAN SOLDIERS WERE KILLED.

I CAN'T BELIEVE WE'RE GIVING GROUND!
IT'S A *TACTICAL RETREAT,* LADS. DON'T MAKE IT EASY FOR 'EM!

WE'RE UNSTOPPABLE!
ONWARD TO PARIS!

CHAPTER 13
THE STEAMROLLER
AUGUST 23, 1914
EASTERN FRONT, GERMANY
SAVE YOUR BULLETS FOR WHEN THINGS GET SERIOUS!
THIS ISN'T SERIOUS?

BUT HOW WILL WE ATTACK?
BAYONETS!

OUR SUPPLY LINES ARE STRETCHED TOO THIN. MORE AMMO WILL ARRIVE SOON.
FOR NOW, CHARGE!

THEY'RE RUNNING! THE GERMANS ARE RUNNING!
SEE? THE BAYONET WORKS! AND YOU DON'T EVEN HAVE TO RELOAD IT.

THE RUSSIANS ARE CRUSHING US. WE NEED MORE TROOPS.
HERE COMES A CAR!
MAYBE THEY HAVE NEWS ABOUT BACKUP.

ANY NEWS OF REINFORCEMENTS?
YES. THESE ARE THEM, GENERALS HINDENBURG AND LUDENDORFF.

TWO MEN? OUR REINFORCEMENTS ARE TWO MEN!?
GOOD MORNING.
HELLO.
HEY! IT'S THE GUY WHO KNOCKED ON THAT DOOR!

TWO MEN--
IS THIS A JOKE!?
WE'RE DOOMED.
THEY CAN'T SEND TROOPS--EVERY-ONE IS NEEDED FOR THE ATTACK ON PARIS!

HINDENBURG CAME OUT OF RETIREMENT TO JOIN THIS BATTLE.
THAT FILLS ME WITH CONFIDENCE.

AND LUDENDORFF TOOK CARE OF THE FORTS AT LIÉGE WITH EASE!
THAT WAS AGAINST BELGIUM'S CHOCOLATE ARMY.

THIS IS AGAINST THE RUSSIAN STEAMROLLER.
YEAH. WE'RE DOOMED.

GENERAL LUDENDORFF, SIR, HOFFMAN'S SIGNAL CORPS JUST INTERCEPTED THIS.
GOOD HEAVENS! IT'S THE ENTIRE RUSSIAN BATTLE PLAN! IS THIS REAL?

ALL OF TOMORROW'S MANEUVERS ARE HERE! THEY ARE LOW ON AMMO AND SUPPLY LINES ARE STRETCHED TOO THIN...
THIS IS EVERYTHING!

WHERE DID THIS COME FROM?
THE RUSSIANS ARE SENDING THEIR TELEGRAMS OUT OVER THE WIRELESS UNCODED.

UNCODED!? DID THEY MAKE ANY EFFORT AT SECURITY?
THEY SENT THE TELEGRAM LATE AT NIGHT. I SUPPOSE THEY THOUGHT WE WERE ALL ASLEEP.

WE ARE OUTNUMBERED HERE, BUT THE RUSSIANS HAVE JUST SHOWN US THEIR WEAKNESS. IT'S TECHNOLOGY.
WE HAVE SECURE COMMUNICTIONS; THEY DON'T. WE HAVE HIGH-SPEED RAILWAY TROOP TRANSPORT; THEY DON'T. WE'LL ALWAYS BE ONE STEP AHEAD OF THEM.

WE'LL ENCIRCLE THEM AND WIPE THEM OFF THE MAP.

AUGUST 1914
THE BATTLE OF TANNENBERG
LOOK! GERMAN CAVALRY!
MOVE OUT!
I'M STARVING! I HAVEN'T EATEN IN THREE DAYS!
NO, THE GERMANS ARE OVER *HERE*!
THEY'RE MOVING FAST! I'M GLAD THEY DON'T HAVE ARTILLERY.
THAT'S ARTILLERY!
RETREAT! BACK ACROSS THE BORDER!
ANNIHILATE THEM!
WE HAVE DONE IT! WE'VE ENCIRCLED THE RUSSIANS!
WE ARE SURROUNDED!
KEEP FIRING! KEEP FIRING!
WITH WHAT? I'M OUT OF BULLETS.
THE RUSSIAN INVADERS WERE DEFEATED AT TANNENBERG. **80,000** RUSSIAN SOLDIERS WERE KILLED, **100,000** WERE CAPTURED.
GERMANY WON THE BATTLE WITH **12,000** CASUALTIES.
WE OUTSMARTED A VASTLY SUPERIOR FORCE FOR A **SMASHING** VICTORY!
WORD FROM THE WESTERN FRONT--THEY ARE SENDING REINFORCEMENTS AT LAST!
OH, SURE. ***NOW*** THEY SEND 'EM!

CHAPTER
14
"PROTECT PARIS!"
ATTACK AND RETREAT!
ATTACK AND RETREAT!

CUT THESE TELEGRAPH WIRES.
BLOW UP THESE TRAIN TRACKS.
THIS IS MY HOMETOWN --WE USE THESE RAILROADS.

DO YOU WANT THE GERMANS TO HAVE THEM?
BLOW THEM UP!

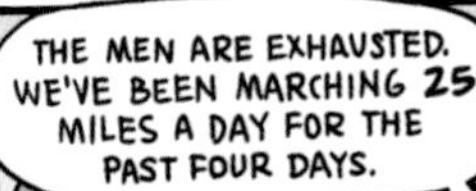
THE MEN ARE EXHAUSTED. WE'VE BEEN MARCHING **25** MILES A DAY FOR THE PAST FOUR DAYS.

KEEP THEM MARCHING! WE ARE ALMOST TO **PARIS**!

MEANWHILE, IN PARIS...
WE SHOULD LEAVE!
THEY BURNED LOUVAIN--THEY'LL BURN **PARIS**, TOO!

CURSE ZOSE EAGLES! I HATE ZEM SO MUCH!
STOP SHOUTING AND START DIGGING! WE NEED TO BUILD DEFENSES!

I BROUGHT MY OWN SPADE.
WE'LL NEED 10,000 MORE JUST LIKE IT.

BARRICADE ALL ENTRANCES TO THE CITY--
EVEN THE **SEWERS**!

LET'S SEE ZOSE EAGLES GET THROUGH **ZAT**!

WIRE EVERY BRIDGE WITH EXPLOSIVES.
BUT, THIS BRIDGE IS A WORK OF **ART**!

HOPEFULLY THE GERMANS WON'T GET THIS FAR.

FOOM
SACRÉ BLEU!
WHAT WAS THAT?

THEY ARE DROPPING BOMBS FROM THAT FILTHY AEROPLANE!

THE WORLD'S CENTER OF ART AND CULTURE--AND THEY DROP **BOMBS** ON HER!
WE'RE PUTTING OUR PLANE TO BETTER USE--AS A ***SPY PLANE***.

I DON'T BELIEVE IT! THE GERMANS AREN'T MARCHING TO PARIS--THEY ARE GOING SOUTHEAST OF THE CITY. AND VON KLUCK'S FLANK IS **WIDE OPEN**.
BREGUET AG. 4

I UNDERSTAND THE NEED TO MAKE THE COUNTRIES ANIMALS, BUT MUST WE GIVE THE GENERALS SILLY NAMES?
ALEXANDER VON KLUCK COMMANDS THE GERMAN 1ST ARMY. THAT'S HIS REAL NAME.

SOUTHEAST OF PARIS? WHY WOULD VON KLUCK DO THAT?
HE WANTS TO **SURROUND** OUR ARMIES--THE GERMAN GENERALS LOVE ENCIRCLEMENT.

WE HAVE TO TAKE ADVANTAGE OF THIS GAP.
WE ATTACK **NOW**--WITH EVERYTHING WE'VE GOT!

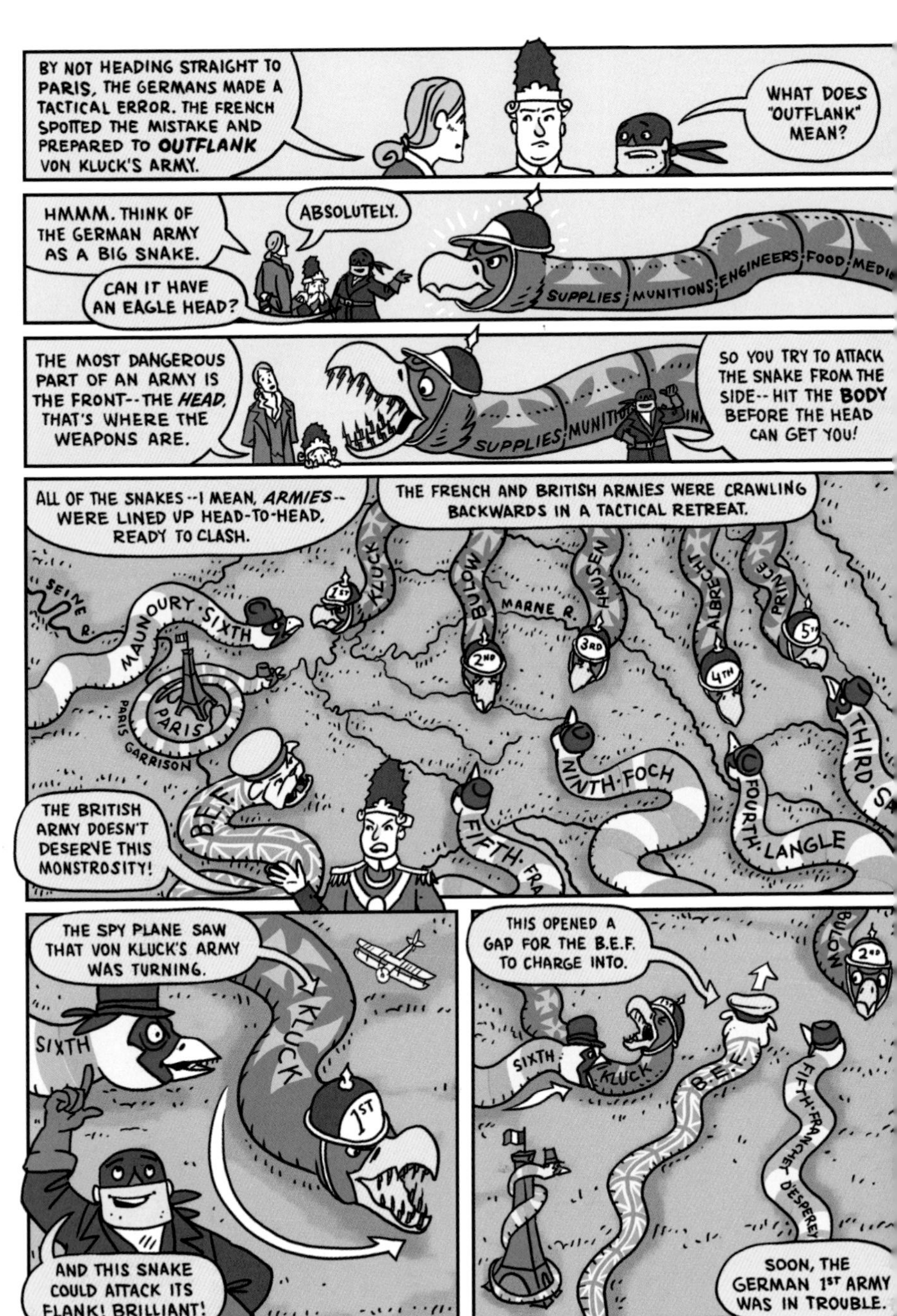
BY NOT HEADING STRAIGHT TO PARIS, THE GERMANS MADE A TACTICAL ERROR. THE FRENCH SPOTTED THE MISTAKE AND PREPARED TO OUTFLANK VON KLUCK'S ARMY.
WHAT DOES "OUTFLANK" MEAN?
HMMM. THINK OF THE GERMAN ARMY AS A BIG SNAKE.
ABSOLUTELY.
CAN IT HAVE AN EAGLE HEAD?
SUPPLIES
MUNITIONS
ENGINEERS
FOOD
THE MOST DANGEROUS PART OF AN ARMY IS THE FRONT--THE HEAD. THAT'S WHERE THE WEAPONS ARE.
SUPPLIES
SO YOU TRY TO ATTACK THE SNAKE FROM THE SIDE--HIT THE BODY BEFORE THE HEAD CAN GET YOU!
ALL OF THE SNAKES--I MEAN, ARMIES--WERE LINED UP HEAD-TO-HEAD, READY TO CLASH.
THE FRENCH AND BRITISH ARMIES WERE CRAWLING BACKWARDS IN A TACTICAL RETREAT.
SEINE R.
MAUNOURY SIXTH
PARIS
PARIS GARRISON
KLUCK
1ST
BULOW
2ND
MARNE R.
HAUSEN
3RD
ALBRECHT
4TH
PRINCE
5TH
NINTH·FOCH
FOURTH·LANGLE
FIFTH
B.E.F.
THE BRITISH ARMY DOESN'T DESERVE THIS MONSTROSITY!
THE SPY PLANE SAW THAT VON KLUCK'S ARMY WAS TURNING.
SIXTH
KLUCK
1ST
AND THIS SNAKE COULD ATTACK ITS FLANK! BRILLIANT!
THIS OPENED A GAP FOR THE B.E.F. TO CHARGE INTO.
BULOW
2ND
SIXTH
KLUCK
B.E.F.
FIFTH·FRANCHET D'ESPEREY
SOON, THE GERMAN 1ST ARMY WAS IN TROUBLE.

CHAPTER 15
THE TAXIS OF THE MARNE
"THE MOMENT HAS PASSED FOR LOOKING TO THE REAR."
GENERAL JOSEPH JOFFRE
"ALL OUR EFFORTS MUST BE DIRECTED TO ATTACKING AND DRIVING BACK THE ENEMY!"

"TROOPS WHO CAN ADVANCE NO FURTHER MUST, AT ANY PRICE, HOLD ON TO THE GROUND THEY HAVE CONQUERED AND DIE ON THE SPOT RATHER THAN GIVE WAY."

MAUNOURY'S SIXTH ARMY WILL TAKE HEAVY CASUALTIES. THEY'LL BE ALONE AGAINST VON KLUCK'S ARMY.
THERE IS NO WAY TO GET B.E.F. OR FIFTH ARMY REINFORCEMENTS TO THEM.

THE GOOD NEWS IS: VON KLUCK HAS GIVEN US AN OPENING-- WE CAN STOP THE GERMAN ADVANCE!
THE BAD NEWS IS: WE'RE ON OUR OWN.

WE WILL FIGHT TO THE LAST MAN!
FOR PARIS!

WHAT IS THAT?
IT'S A TAXI-- A PARIS TAXI!

IT'S THE PARIS RESERVES! REINFORCEMENTS, BY TAXICAB!
PARIS IS SAVED!
PARIS RESERVE GARRISON
6,000 TROOPS, FRESH FROM PARIS IN 600 TAXIS!

THE GERMAN ARMIES WERE DRIVEN BACK FORTY MILES, TO THE AISNE RIVER.
THERE, THEY DID SOMETHING THAT WOULD SET THE TONE FOR THE REST OF THE WAR.
THEY DUG A HOLE.
DIG IN! WE'LL FIGHT THEM FROM A PREPARED POSITION --A TRENCH!
WE'LL DIG IN TOO!
EVERYONE DIG!
THE TRENCHES GREW DEEPER--AND LONGER, WITH EACH SIDE DIGGING IN A RACE TO THE SEA.
GERMAN TRENCH
FRENCH, B.E.F. TRENCH
AMIENS
NOYON
SOISSONS
CHALENS
BAR LE DUC
VERDUN
METZ
MOUSSON
ST. MICHEL
TOUL
THAT'S SILLY. HOW CAN THEY FIGHT FROM DOWN IN THE GROUND?
THEY LAUNCHED SHELLS AT EACH OTHER,
OR ONE SIDE WOULD TRY TO RUSH THE OTHER.
THE SCORCHED EARTH BETWEEN THE TRENCHES BECAME KNOWN AS "NO-MAN'S-LAND."

CHAPTER
16
THE KING'S FLOOD
ANTWERP, BELGIUM
OCTOBER 1914
BEHIND THEIR TRENCHES THE GERMAN ARMY TIGHTENED THEIR GRIP ON BELGIUM.
HELLO? KING ALBERT, ARE YOU IN THERE?
THE BIG GUNS ARE HERE.
WE DESTROYED YOUR FORTS AT LIÈGE AND NAMUR--WE'LL FLATTEN YOUR FORTS IN ANTWERP TOO!
NOTHING CAN WITHSTAND OUR **BIG BERTHAS**!
THE BELGIANS ARE FLEEING! ANTWERP IS OURS!
RUN AWAY, CHOCOLATE SOLDIERS!
WHERE IS KING ALBERT?
HE'S WITH THE LAST OF HIS RAGGED ARMY.
FOR GENERATIONS, BELGIAN DAMS HAVE HELD BACK THE SEA.
TODAY, WE ***RELEASE THE OCEAN!***
OPEN THE SLUICE GATES. WE WILL ***FLOOD*** THE GERMAN INVADERS.
SIR, THE CIVILIANS HAVE FLED THE AREA. WE DON'T KNOW HOW TO WORK THE FLOODGATES.
WE STAYED BEHIND. WE'LL HELP YOU DROWN THOSE EAGLES.
IT'LL TAKE THREE OR FOUR NIGHTS TO OPEN ALL THE GATES.
WE'LL OPEN THEM AT HIGH TIDE.
IS IT RAINING?
IT'S UP TO MY KNEES.
IT'S UP TO MY SHOULDERS!
TRY CROSSING NOW! THIS RIVER'S A MILE WIDE!
WE WILL GET YOU SOONER OR LATER, KING ALBERT!

CHAPTER 17
THE FIRST BATTLE OF YPRES
WE'VE DUG OUR WAY BACK TO BELGIUM!
THE TOWN AHEAD, YPRES, IS THE ONLY THING BETWEEN OUR PORTS AND THE GERMANS.
WHOEVER CONTROLS YPRES CONTROLS BELGIUM'S PORTS.
THANK YOU FOR COMING TO OUR AID. WE'VE BEEN CHASED TO THE EDGE OF OUR COUNTRY.
WE'LL MAKE OUR STAND HERE.
WE WILL HOLD THE LINE. THE GERMANS WON'T TAKE YPRES.
LANGEMARCK
STEADY RIFLE FIRE, LADS. THEY'RE SENDING RAW VOLUNTEERS AT US!
YPRES
REINFORCEMENTS HAVE ARRIVED! FROM INDIA!
YIPPERS?
WI-PERS?
EYE-PRESS?
IT'S PRONOUNCED "EEP"
WE'RE FLEEING TO FRANCE.
BELGIUM ISN'T SAFE FOR BELGIANS ANYMORE!
I DON'T UNDERSTAND ANYONE'S TACTICS. THEY ALL SEEM TO BE RUNNING ABOUT HELTER-SKELTER!

YPRES IS THE LAST GAP INTO FRANCE. WE MUST CHARGE THROUGH WHILE WE CAN.
IF WE TAKE THE PORTS, THE ENGLISH WON'T HAVE SEA ACCESS TO BELGIUM!
PASSCHENDAELE
DOES EVERY B.E.F. SOLDIER HAVE A MACHINE GUN?!
WE'VE GOT A FEW HUNDRED GERMAN PRISONERS--WHERE DO WE TAKE THEM?
WE'RE OUT OF MEN AND AMMO. WE'RE AT THE END OF OUR ROPE!
I DON'T THINK THE GERMANS KNOW.
SHELL THOSE TALL TOWERS! THE FRENCH ARE USING THEM TO SPY ON US!
WE NEED EVERYONE--COOKS, CLERKS, MESSENGERS--WE NEED EVERY LAST MAN TO HOLD THESE WOODS!
WHAT'S GOING ON IN THERE? WE'VE SENT IN THREE BATTALIONS!
POLYGON WOOD
HOOGE
ATTACK!
GHELUVELT
SANCTUARY WOOD
RETREAT! WE'RE OUTNUMBERED!
BUT THERE'S ONLY A FEW--
THAT'S JUST THE ADVANCE FORCE!

THE BATTLE RAGED FOR FIVE WEEKS
THE GERMAN ADVANCE ON YPRES WAS HALTED.
THE RACE TO THE SEA WAS OVER.
LANGEMARCK
25,000 GERMAN STUDENT VOLUNTEERS WERE KILLED IN LANGEMARCK, THE BATTLE WAS CALLED THE *KINDERMORD,* THE *"MASSACRE OF THE INNOCENTS."*
YPRES
THE **CLOTH HALL**, BUILT IN THE 1300s, WAS REDUCED TO RUBBLE.
THE ARMIES AT YPRES PAID A TERRIBLE PRICE.
FRENCH • KILLED, WOUNDED OR MISSING: 85,000
BELGIAN • KILLED, WOUNDED OR MISSING: 21,000

PASSCHENDAELE

THE ORIGINAL B.E.F. WAS ALL BUT DESTROYED. BRITAIN WOULD HAVE TO REPLACE THESE SOLDIERS WITH RAW RECRUITS AND TERRITORIAL FORCES.

THIS STRETCH OF TRENCHES, KNOWN AS THE YPRES SALIENT, WOULD SEE MANY MORE BATTLES.

THE FIGHTING FROZE AS WINTER SETTLED IN.

BOTH SIDES DUG DEEPER INTO THEIR TRENCHES TO WAIT OUT THE COLD STANDSTILL.

POLYGON WOOD

BRITISH • KILLED, WOUNDED OR MISSING: 55,000

GERMAN • KILLED, WOUNDED OR MISSING: 134,000

SO THAT'S IT, THE WAR IS OVER?
NOT A BIT! THEY'VE JUST STOPPED FOR WINTER.
PHEW. I NEED A BREAK TO CATCH UP.
THIS IS ALL TOO MUCH FOR ME.
SO MUCH DEATH AND DESTRUCTION.
SO MUCH RUNNING FROM PLACE TO PLACE. ATTACK, RETREAT, ADVANCE!
I WASN'T CONFUSED, I ENJOY THE DASHING ABOUT!
I AM SORRY TO SAY, MOST OF THE "*DASHING ABOUT*" ENDS HERE.
THIS IS NOW THE WAR OF THE **TRENCHES**.
I HAVEN'T SEEN ANY WOLVES OR GRIFFINS FOR A WHILE--WHAT ARE THEY UP TO?
YES, WHAT'S GOING ON IN SERBIA?
THE AUSTRO-HUNGARIAN ARMY DECIDED NOT TO STOP FOR THE WINTER.
WE WERE TOO HASTY LAST TIME.
NOW WE ARE *PREPARED* TO INVADE SERBIA.
BELGRADE, SERBIA DECEMBER 2, 1914
BELGRADE HAS FALLEN! SERBIA IS **OURS**!
NO, IT ISN'T.
SERBIA WAS READY FOR THE ATTACK. AND ON THEIR HOME GROUND, THEY FOUGHT BACK WITH ***FURY***.
THE AUSTRO-HUNGARIAN ARMY SUFFERED OVER **200,000** CASUALTIES-- **HALF** OF THEIR INVASION FORCE.
IT WAS A CATASTROPHIC DEFEAT.
THE SERBIAN ARMY WON THE BATTLE. BUT WITH 170,000 CASUALTIES,
THEIR ARMY WAS IN FRAGMENTS.
HOLY MOLEY. I THOUGHT WE WERE TAKING A BREAK.

CHAPTER
18
REINFORCEMENTS
SO MANY CASUALTIES! THEY'LL SOON RUN OUT OF SOLDIERS!

EVERYONE WAS RUNNING OUT OF SOLDIERS. ORDERS WERE SENT OUT ACROSS THE WORLD:
SEND REINFORCEMENTS.

TROOPS ARRIVED FROM EVERY CORNER OF THE BRITISH EMPIRE.
MANY WERE ESCORTED BY JAPANESE SHIPS.

FROM AUSTRALIA 20,000

FROM CANADA 40,000

FROM NEW ZEALAND 8,000

FROM INDIA
WE ARE ALREADY HERE. WE FOUGHT AT YPRES!

FRANCE WELCOMED TROOPS FROM COLONIES IN AFRICA.
FROM SENEGAL
WE WERE AT YPRES TOO!

IN THE UNITED KINGDOM, OVER A *MILLION* CIVILIANS VOLUNTEERED FOR SERVICE.
WANTS YOU
JOIN YOUR COUNTRY'S ARMY!

RECRUIT

DID ANYONE JOIN GERMANY?
YES, YOUR FRIENDS, TURKEY, OTHERWISE KNOWN AS THE OTTOMAN EMPIRE, JOINED THE CENTRAL POWERS.

I GET IT, *OTTER*-MAN EMPIRE.
JOLLY GOOD.

KANGAROO, BEAVER, KIWI, TIGER, BUFFALO, AND OTTER.
STILL NO *BUNNY*.

WHAT ANIMAL IS JAPAN?
YOU SAID JAPANESE SHIPS ESCORTED THE REINFORCEMENTS.
JAPAN IS REPRESENTED BY TANUKI-- THE RACCOON DOG.
THAT'S *ADORABLE*!
JAPAN'S INVOLVEMENT IN THE WAR WAS PRIMARILY NAVAL-BASED.
THIS WAR'S BEEN SHORT ON NAVAL ACTION SO FAR.
HERE'S A NAVY STORY.
IF BRITANNIA RULES THE WAVES, WE MUST GO *UNDER* THE WAVES.
HUH?
BEHOLD, THE *UNTERSEEBOOT*!
SPLOOSH
WE WILL SINK THEIR FLEET FROM BENEATH
WITH THIS *ONE* LITTLE BOAT?
WE HAVE **29** OF THEM.
SPLOOOOOOOOOOOSH
THAT'S CHEATING! YOU CAN'T GO *UNDE* THE SEA!
THE GERMAN **U-BOATS** DID.
AND THEY WERE VERY SUCCESSFUL.
HOW DID THEY HOLD THEIR BREATH FOR SO LONG?

GERMAN U-BOATS ROAMED THE DEEP. THE BRITISH NAVY PATROLLED THE WAVES. ARMIES OF MILLIONS FROZE IN THEIR TRENCHES.

THE YEAR ENDED, BUT THE WAR DID NOT.

WHO'S WINNING?

1915

NO ONE BUT THE GOD OF WAR.

ENJOYING THIS, **ARES?**

HE'S GOTTEN UGLIER SINCE WE LAST SAW HIM.

CHAPTER
TRENCH 19 LOCKED
I DIDN'T KNOW WE'D HAVE TO *LIVE* IN THESE HOLES.
DIG, DIG, DIG! WE'LL TURN OUR TRENCH INTO AN UNDERGROUND FORTRESS.
MUD AND BLOOD AND NEVER ENOUGH SHELLS.
PLENTY OF SHELLS, BUT THE GERMANS HAVE THEM ALL.
THERE HAS TO BE AN EASIER WAY TO KILL THE FRENCH.
NEW UNIFORMS. NO MORE RED PANTALOONS.
I LIKED THE RED PANTALOONS.
THE NEW FRENCH HELMET IS MADE OF STEEL. IT IS CALLED "*THE ADRIAN*."
THIS IS OURS.
IT'S CALLED "*HELMET, MARK I.*"
CAN I HAVE A FRENCH ONE?
EVERYONE IS GETTING *STEEL* HELMETS! OURS ARE STILL *LEATHER!* I WANT *STEEL!*
QUIET! YOU WILL WEAR YOUR PICKELHAUBE AND YOU WILL *LIKE* IT!

DOWN! INCOMING SHELLS!
HEY! WHERE ARE THE ROOSTERS GOING?
GET DOWN, YOU LOT! DON'T RUN IN THE OPEN LIKE THAT!
GAS! GAS! THEY ARE SHOOTING GAS SHELLS!
POISON GAS!
THAT IS THE WORST, MOST DISHONORABLE PIECE OF FIGHTING I HAVE EVER SEEN.
THE PEOPLE OF THE FUTURE ARE BARBARIANS!
WHAT DOES THE GAS DO? DOES IT SMELL BAD?
THE GAS CAUSED A PERSON'S LUNGS TO FILL WITH LIQUID.
IF YOU BREATHED TOO MUCH, YOU COULD DROWN ON DRY GROUND.
BEFORE LONG, BOTH SIDES WERE USING GAS.
PUT ON YOUR HYPO HELMETS.
IT'S TIME TO GIVE THE GERMANS A TASTE OF THEIR OWN MEDICINE.
FIRE!
ATTACK BEFORE THE GAS CLEARS!
I CAN'T BREATHE IN THIS THING!
KEEP YOUR MASK ON!
COUGH
COUGH
COUGH
COUGH
COUGH
COUGH

CHAPTER
20
GALLIPOLI
THE WESTERN FRONT IS AT A STANDSTILL! IT IS TIME TO LAUNCH A NEW CAPAIGN.
WESTERN FRONT
DEADLOCK!
- GAS
- COUNTERATTAC
- RESISTANCE:
- HYPO H
- SMOKE
- MASK
THE OTTOMAN EMPIRE HAS JOINED OUR ENEMIES. THEY COULD BE THE WEAK LINK--AND THE KEY TO WINNING THIS WAR.
THE OTTOMANS CONTROL THE DARDANELLES STRAIGHT.
IT'S A WATER ROUTE TO RUSSIA AND ASIA.
WE COULD SHIP RUSSIAN TROOPS TO THE WESTERN FRONT!
WE COULD SHIP FRESH SUPPLIES TO THE EASTERN FRONT! IT'S A WIN-WIN!
RUSSIA
AUSTRIA-HUNGARY
ROMANIA
BULGARIA
SERBIA
ITALY
ALBANIA
GREECE
DARDANELLES
OTTOMAN EMPIRE
WE CAN'T DO IT. EVERY WARSHIP WE HAVE IS NEEDED TO KEEP GERMANY BLOCKADED.
WE CAN USE OUR OLD, OUT-OF-DATE SHIPS!
OUR RETIRED FLEET IS FAR SUPERIOR TO ANYTHING TURKEY HAS.
WE'LL MAKE QUICK WORK OF THEM!
VERY WELL, MR. CHURCHILL, BRING US THE DARDANELLES.
THEY'VE GOT MINES!
IF OUR SHIPS BUMP ONE OF THOSE... KA-BOOM!
THE NARROWS ARE PACKED WITH 'EM!
IF THE MINES DON'T SINK US, THE FORTS ON SHORE WILL. WE CAN'T GET THROUGH.
GALLIPOLI PENINSULA
DARDANELLES
LET'S DROP TROOPS ON THE TIP OF THIS PENINSULA--THEY CAN CAPTURE THOSE FORTS FROM LAND.

30,000 ALLIED TROOPS, FRENCH, BRITISH, AND ANZAC WERE TAKEN TO THE GALLIPOLI PENINSULA.
WHAT IS ANZAC?
THE AUSTRALIAN AND NEW ZEALAND ARMY CORPS.
I'LL TAKE THIS OVER MUDDY TRENCHES ANY DAY!
TOO RIGHT!
SOME TROOPS LANDED SAFELY.
ZIS BEACH, SHE IS MAGNIFIQUE!
SOME NEVER MADE IT ASHORE.
RIVER CLYDE
RACE ACROSS THE BRIDGE OF BOATS--
BUT WE'RE RIGHT UNDER THE TURKISH GUNS!
SAVE US! THE OCEAN'S RED WITH BLOOD!
THE ONES WHO MADE IT ASHORE DUG IN DEEP.
HUNDREDS OF MILES BY SEA AND WE'RE BACK IN A TRENCH.

WE WILL FIGHT UNTIL THESE INVADERS ARE GONE FROM OUR SHORES!
BUT WE'RE COMPLETELY OUT OF AMMO!
THEN WE CHARGE WITH BAYONETS.
I DO NOT ORDER YOU TO FIGHT. I ORDER YOU TO *DIE*.
GOOD HEAVENS! THOSE OTTOMAN SOLDIERS ARE A BRAVE LOT!
THEY ARE. THIS REGIMENT, THE *TURKISH 57TH*, FOUGHT UNTIL EVERY SINGLE MAN WAS DEAD OR WOUNDED.
BEFORE LONG, THE FORCES AT GALLIPOLI WERE LOCKED IN TRENCH COMBAT.
OVER THE TOP, MATES!
THE ALLIED FORCES CHARGED AGAIN AND AGAIN. THEY GAINED LITTLE GROUND.
THE OTTOMAN EMPIRE'S ARMY GREW AND GREW.
U-BOATS ARRIVED AND BEGAN SINKING CHURCHILL'S FLEET.
OY! WHAT'S HAP'NIN' TO THE BOATS!?
DON'T LEAVE US HERE!
AFTER EIGHT MONTHS OF HARD FIGHTING, AND 250,000 CASUALTIES,
THE ALLIES WITHDREW FROM GALLIPOLI.
VICTORY FOR THE OTTOMAN EMPIRE!
VICTORY FOR TURKEY!

CHAPTER 21
COLLAPSE AND RETREAT
MAY 1, 1915 EASTERN FRONT
BAD NEWS. WE ARE OUT OF GUNS.
OUT OF SOLDIERS?

NO, WE HAVE MILLIONS OF SOLDIERS--WE HAVE NO GUNS FOR THEM.
SEND THEM OUT ANYWAY.

WHEN'S MY TURN WITH THE RIFLE?
WHEN I DIE, YOU GET THE RIFLE.
WHEN YOU DIE, HE GETS THE RIFLE.

WE'RE STILL GETTING RADIO INFO FROM RUSSIA. IT APPEARS THEY ARE OUT OF GUNS.
NO GUNS?
AUSTRIA-HUNGARY COULD USE A VICTORY OR TWO. THEY MIGHT BE ABLE TO WIN AGAINST A WEAPONLESS ARMY--MAYBE.

GERMANY TEAMED UP WITH AUSTRIA-HUNGARY. TOGETHER, THEY INVADED RUSSIA.
THEY WERE MERCILESS.

STAND AND FIGHT!
FOR RUSSIA!

THEY DIDN'T STAND. THE BEARS WERE PUSHED BACK HUNDREDS OF MILES INTO RUSSIA.
1915 IS NOT A GOOD YEAR FOR THE ALLIES.

CHAPTER 22
THE LUSITANIA
MAY 7, 1915
NORTH ATLANTIC
18 KILOMETERS OFF THE IRISH COAST AND CLOSING, CAPTAIN.
TARGET IS IN SIGHT. IT HAS FOUR SMOKESTACKS.
FOUR, EH? SHE'S A BIG ONE.
BIG AND FAST. WE'D NEVER CATCH HER IN OPEN WATER.
FOUR STACKS--IT MAY BE THE LUSITANIA. IS SHE IN RANGE?
SHE WON'T BE FOR LONG.
LUSITANIA IS LISTED AS... AN ARMED MERCHANT CRUISER--A TARGET!
IT LOOKS LIKE A PASSENGER LINER TO ME.
SHE CARRIES MORE THAN PASSENGERS--SHE'S LOADED WITH AMMUNITION FOR THE WESTERN FRONT.
SINK HER.
SSSSSSS
FIRE TORPEDOES!
BOOOM
WHAT WAS THAT?
AN EXPLOSION! MAN THE LIFEBOATS!
OUT OF MY WAY!
BOARD CAREFULLY--THERE'S ROOM FOR EVERYONE!
WE'RE GOING DOWN TOO FAST!
THE RMS LUSITANIA SUNK WITH 1,198 SOULS. THE SHIP WENT DOWN SO QUICKLY, ONLY SIX OF THE 48 LIFEBOATS WERE LAUNCHED IN TIME.
OF THE 1,198 PASSENGERS WHO DIED, 128 WERE AMERICANS.
THIS IS A SERIOUS BREACH OF NAVAL ETIQUETTE--SINKING A PASSENGER SHIP!
THE LUSITANIA WAS CARRYING SHIPMENTS OF RIFLES AND SHELLS. SHE WAS A LEGITIMATE TARGET.
STILL, TO KILL A THOUSAND CIVILIANS--IT'S NOT VERY SPORTING.

CHAPTER 23
MOUNTAIN BATTLES
WE OUTNUMBER THE AUSTRO-HUNGARIANS THREE TO ONE!
WE DECLARE WAR!
HEY! A KITTY-CAT! WHO'S THAT?
ITALY. TECHNICALLY, ITALY'S NATIONAL ANIMAL IS THE WOLF BUT
--SERBIA!
WE'LL ATTACK THROUGH THE MOUNTAINS. INTO THE ALPS!
GET READY TO CLIMB!
ITALIAN SOLDIERS ARE APPROACHING OUR MOUNTAIN BASES!
PREPARE TO FIRE!
FWAM
ARE WE WINNING?
I THINK WE ARE... WE'RE ACTUALLY BEATING SOMEBODY--BY OURSELVES!
YOU WOULDN'T BE SO TOUGH IF YOU WEREN'T ON TOP OF THE MOUNTAINS!
LET'S ATTACK SOMEWHERE ELSE.
KEEP TRYING, KITTY-CATS!
THEY ARE SO MUCH EASIER THAN WOLVES OR BEARS!
GRRRRR.

CHAPTER
24
SERBIA VS. EVERYONE
THE AUSTRO-HUNGARIANS ARE BACK! I CAN'T BELIEVE IT!
WILL THEY NEVER LEARN?

UH-OH, THEY ARE BRINGING THE GERMANS WITH THEM.
YIKES! WE'RE GONNA NEED HELP!

GREECE WILL HELP!
OOH! THE MYTHICAL PHOENIX!

NO! GREECE WILL NOT HELP! GREECE IS NEUTRAL!
BOP
KING CONSTANTINE

WE'LL HELP YOU, SERBIA!
WE'RE ON OUR WAY HOME FROM GALLIPOLI. WE'LL STOP AND LEND OUR SUPPORT.

GREECE IS A FRIENDLY NATION, WE'LL UNLOAD TROOPS AND MARCH ACROSS TO SERBIA.
I DUNNO, ISN'T THIS SORT OF WHAT GERMANY WANTED TO TRY WITH BELGIUM?

HOLD IT RIGHT THERE, YOU DOGS! GREECE IS NEUTRAL!
I WILL NOT LET YOU MARCH THROUGH GREECE.

BUT WE HAVE TO HELP SERBIA!
YOU'LL HAVE TO FIND ANOTHER WAY. GREECE IS CLOSED.

THIS IS THE ONLY WAY TO REACH SERBIA!
TOO BAD.

THE BRITISH WON'T MAKE IT. WE'RE ON OUR OWN.
WE'VE BEATEN THEM BEFORE. WE'LL JUST HAVE TO DO IT AGAIN.
IT'S NOT JUST GERMANY AND AUSTRIA-HUNGARY.
AUSTRIA-HUNGARY
ROMANIA
SERBIA
MONTENEGRO
BULGARIA
GREECE
BULGARIA'S ATTACKING FROM THE EAST!
WE TRIED!
BACK IN 1912, SERBIA TEAMED UP WITH GREECE TO STAB US IN THE BACK. WE LOST THE SECOND BALKAN WAR--WE WON'T LOSE THIS WAR!
HA-HA! BULL-GARIANS.
AUSTRIA-HUNGARY'S ENEMIES ARE OUR ENEMIES.
YOUR DAYS ARE NUMBERED, SERBIA.
IT'S TIME FOR PAYBACK, WOLVES.
IT WAS THE THIRD INVASION OF SERBIA SINCE THE WAR BEGAN.
THIS TIME, IT WORKED.
THE LAST OF SERBIA'S ARMY RETREATED TO MONTENEGRO. AS MANY AS 200,000 DIED IN THE SNOW.
BY THE END OF 1915, ONE-SIXTH OF SERBIA'S ENTIRE POPULATION WAS DEAD.

THE ARMIES ON THE WESTERN FRONT SETTLED IN FOR THEIR SECOND WINTER.
BACK IN 1914, THE KAISER TOLD US ALL WE'D BE HOME BEFORE THE LEAVES FELL.

THEY'VE FALLEN TWICE NOW.

YOU FRESH RECRUITS WO
BELIEVE IT, BUT LAST YEAR
HAD A CHRISTMAS TRUC

WE SANG SONGS AND TRADED GIFTS WITH THE GERMANS.
WE EVEN KICKED A BALL AROUND OUT IN NO-MAN'S-LAND.

DO YOU THINK THERE WILL BE A CHRISTMAS TRUCE THIS YEAR?

LET'S SEE...

P'TING
IT DOESN'T LOOK VERY LIKELY.

OUR GOD OF WAR
S GROWING. EACH
YEAR HE LEARNS
MORE, BECOMES
STRONGER,
BECOMES
WORSE.
YE GODS!
LOOK AT THAT
BRUTE!
HE'S SMOKING
LIKE A CHIMNEY--
AND HE SMELLS
TERRIBLE!
1916

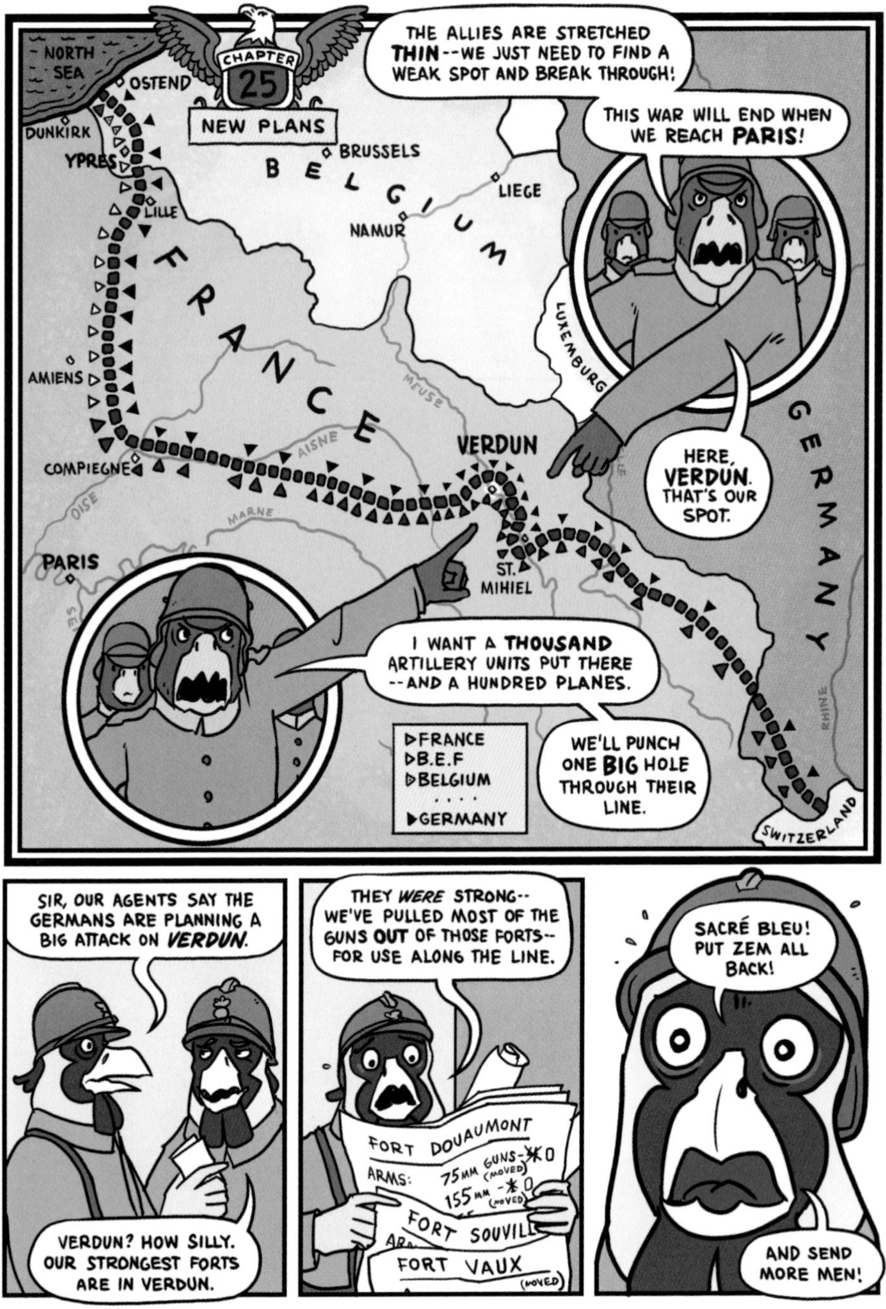

CHAPTER 25

NEW PLANS

NORTH SEA
OSTEND
DUNKIRK
YPRES
LILLE
BRUSSELS
BELGIUM
LIEGE
NAMUR
FRANCE
LUXEMBURG
MEUSE
AMIENS
AISNE
VERDUN
GERMANY
COMPIEGNE
OISE
MARNE
PARIS
ST. MIHIEL
RHINE
SWITZERLAND

THE ALLIES ARE STRETCHED **THIN**--WE JUST NEED TO FIND A WEAK SPOT AND BREAK THROUGH!

THIS WAR WILL END WHEN WE REACH **PARIS**!

HERE, **VERDUN**. THAT'S OUR SPOT.

I WANT A **THOUSAND** ARTILLERY UNITS PUT THERE --AND A HUNDRED PLANES.

WE'LL PUNCH ONE **BIG** HOLE THROUGH THEIR LINE.

▷FRANCE
▷B.E.F
▷BELGIUM
. . . .
▶GERMANY

SIR, OUR AGENTS SAY THE GERMANS ARE PLANNING A BIG ATTACK ON *VERDUN*.
VERDUN? HOW SILLY. OUR STRONGEST FORTS ARE IN VERDUN.

THEY *WERE* STRONG-- WE'VE PULLED MOST OF THE GUNS **OUT** OF THOSE FORTS-- FOR USE ALONG THE LINE.
FORT DOUAUMONT
ARMS: 75MM GUNS-*0 (MOVED)
155MM -*0 (MOVED)
FORT SOUVILL
FORT VAUX
(MOVED)

SACRÉ BLEU! PUT ZEM ALL BACK!
AND SEND MORE MEN!

IN FEBRURY 1916, THE SHELLING OF VERDUN BEGAN.
STORM TROOPERS, YOU WILL BE THE SHOCK TROOPS. RUSH IN AFTER THE BARRAGE AND INFILTRATE THE TRENCHES.
KILL EVERYONE WHO SURVIVES THE BARRAGE.
IT LOOKS LIKE THE GERMANS FINALLY GOT STEEL HELMETS.
AND STEEL SHIRTS!
TEN HOURS OF SHELLING? IS ANYONE LEFT?
SOME OF US. WHAT A NIGHTMARE.
TEN HOURS-- THIS IS A NEW RECORD.
HERE THEY COME!
WHAT!? THE GERMANS ARE COMING--WITH FIRE!
SAY HELLO TO OUR NEW INVENTION--THE FLAMETHROWER!
STORM TROOPERS, ATTACK! GRENADES! GRENADES! GRENADES!
FALL BACK! FALL BACK!

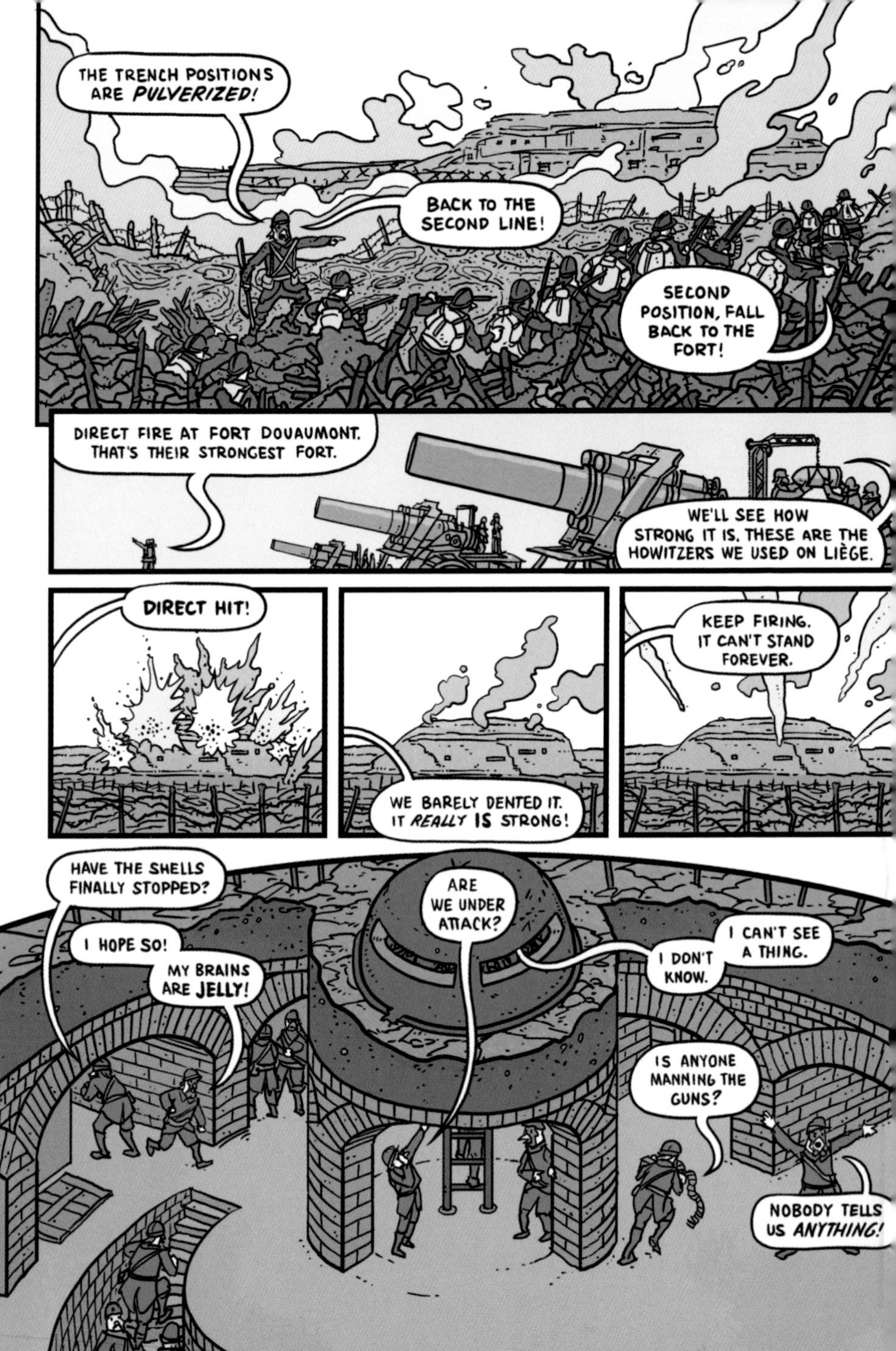
THE TRENCH POSITIONS ARE *PULVERIZED!*
BACK TO THE SECOND LINE!
SECOND POSITION, FALL BACK TO THE FORT!
DIRECT FIRE AT FORT DOUAUMONT. THAT'S THEIR STRONGEST FORT.
WE'LL SEE HOW STRONG IT IS. THESE ARE THE HOWITZERS WE USED ON LIÈGE.
DIRECT HIT!
WE BARELY DENTED IT. IT *REALLY* **IS** STRONG!
KEEP FIRING. IT CAN'T STAND FOREVER.
HAVE THE SHELLS FINALLY STOPPED?
I HOPE SO!
MY BRAINS ARE **JELLY**!
ARE WE UNDER ATTACK?
I DON'T KNOW.
I CAN'T SEE A THING.
IS ANYONE MANNING THE GUNS?
NOBODY TELLS US *ANYTHING!*

WE CAN SQUEEZE IN THROUGH HERE--NOBODY'S GUARDING THIS FORT.
ARE YOU KIDDING? I'M NOT GOING IN THERE.
WHERE IS EVERYONE? THEY DON'T HAVE ANY GUNS. HAVE THE FRENCH LEFT FORT DOUAUMONT?
AAAAAK! A GERMAN IS IN ZE FORT!
SSH!
HOW MANY SOLDIERS HOLD THIS FORT?
SIXTY.
FRANCE'S STRONGEST FORT AND THEY MAN IT WITH SIXTY OLD-TIMERS.
NICE WORK, SEARGENT KUNZE.
WE'LL ALL GET MEDALS FOR THIS!
BRING EVERYTHING! FORT DOUAUMONT IS CAPTURED! THE COLONEL IS DEAD! THE COMMANDERS ARE ALL DEAD!
'ALLO?
'ALLO?
THE WIRE'S DEAD, TOO!
IT WILL BE EASY TO HOLD THIS FORT, BUT WE'LL HAVE TO BRING IN OUR OWN GUNS.
EASIER SAID THAN DONE.
GENERAL PÉTAIN, THE GERMANS HOLD FORT DOUAUMONT! IF THEY TAKE ANY MORE FORTS, VERDUN WILL BE LOST!
YOU MUST HOLD THEM OFF!
ILS NE PASSERONT PAS!
*THEY SHALL NOT PASS!

FOLLOW THIS ROAD TO VERDUN.
KEEP THEM ROLLING. WE NEED EVERY TRUCK IN FRANCE ON THIS ROAD, CARRYING EVERY MAN, EVERY GUN, AND EVERY *BULLET* WE CAN GET.
Verdun →
La Voie Sacrée
* THE SACRED PATH
THE FRENCH POURED RESOURCES INTO VERDUN. THREE-QUARTERS OF THE FRENCH ARMY WOULD SERVE IN VERDUN AT ONE POINT OR ANOTHER.
THE GERMANS ARE USING *PHOSGENE* GAS NOW--IT'S *TEN* TIMES DEADLIER THAN LAST YEAR'S CHLORINE GAS.
I HOPE THESE NEW MASKS WORK.
SO FAR, SO GOOD.
FORT DOUAUMONT WILL BE OURS AGAIN!
NEVER!
WHO WON AT VERDUN?
THE BATTLE OF VERDUN HAS ONLY JUST BEGUN.
YOU'LL HAVE TO WAIT AND SEE.

CHAPTER 26
JUTLAND CLASH
NORTH SEA, MAY 31, 1916
THIS WAR DOESN'T HAVE *NEARLY* ENOUGH NAVAL BATTLES!
FUNNY YOU SHOULD MENTION IT. THERE WAS A MAJOR NAVY BATTLE IN 1916:
THE BATTLE OF JUTLAND.
OOH! SOUNDS IMPRESSIVE!
THE GERMAN *IMPERIAL HIGH SEAS FLEET* FOUGHT THE BRITISH *ROYAL NAVY'S GRAND FLEET* IN THE ICY WATERS OF THE NORTH SEA.
THE GERMANS HAD 99 SHIPS,
THE BRITISH HAD 151.
SOUNDS LIKE AN EASY VICTORY, TELL ON.
FOR TWO DAYS, THESE MASSIVE FLEETS BLASTED AWAY AT EACH OTHER.
YES! YES! PROPER WARFARE AT **LAST**--BROADSIDES AT SEA!
THE ROYAL FLEET SANK ELEVEN SHIPS.
IN THE END, BOTH SIDES DECLARED VICTORY.
IT WAS THE ONLY LARGE FLEET BATTLE OF WWI.
THE GERMANS SANK *FOURTEEN* SHIPS.

CHAPTER 27
THE SOMME
SOMME RIVER, FRANCE JUNE, 1916
WE NEED TO TAKE SOME PRESSURE OFF OF THE FRENCH AT VERDUN.
YES, SIR!

YOU ARE NEW UNPROVEN RECRUITS--BUT YOU WILL SOON HAVE A CHANCE TO PROVE YOURSELVES,
HERE, AT THE SOMME.
YES, SIR!

YOU CARRY THE NEWEST GUNS, THE NEWEST ARTILLERY, THE NEWEST GAS MASKS-- WE WILL BE READY FOR THEM!
YES, SIR!

OUR ATTACK WILL DRAW FORCES AWAY FROM VERDUN.
YES, SIR!

TO THE SOMME!

THIS WAS THE LARGEST BRITISH ARMY THE WORLD HAD EVER SEEN--ONE AND A HALF MILLION SOLDIERS.
TO THE SOMME!

ENGLISHMEN, SCOTSMEN, AUSTRALIANS, SOUTH AFRICANS, AND CANADIANS ALL DUG INTO THE MUD OF THE SOMME.
WE 'AVENT GOT A WIFE OR A NICE LITTLE WENCH, BUT WE'RE ALL QUITE 'APPY IN OUR OLD FRENCH TRENCH!

OY! 'AVE YOU SEEN OUR NEW SECRET WEAPON?
LET'S SEE THE GERMANS TRY TO STOP THIS!
IT'S CALLED A TANK.
LOOK AT THAT! WE'LL WIN THE WAR WITH THAT!
THEY'RE BUILT TO ROLL OVER TRENCHES.
WHY IS IT CALLED A "TANK"?
THESE MACHINES WERE A SECRET PROJECT--COOKED UP IN PART BY WINSTON CHURCHILL.
THE ENGINEERS AND FACTORY WORKERS WHO CREATED THEM REFERRED TO THEM AS "WATER TANKS" TO KEEP THEM SECRET.
SAY, WHAT ARE THOSE?
JUST A NEW SORT OF WATER TANK-- THE TROOPS GET THIRSTY, YOU KNOW.
TANKS, EH?
THE NAME STUCK.
A SELF-PROPELLED HEAVY GUN WITH PROTECTIVE ARMOR --IT'S BRILLIANT!
I DON'T LIKE THE NAME. I'D CALL THEM...
"SHELLED-SHOOTERS"!
I CAN'T WAIT TO SEE THEM IN ACTION!
OR HOW ABOUT
"BIG BAD IRONCLADS"?
THE BATTLE OF THE SOMME WAS THE FIRST TIME TANKS WERE USED IN COMBAT.
I'VE GOT IT!
"TURTLE-BANGERS"!

THE SOMME
JUNE 24, 1916
HERE IS THE ATTACK PLAN.
DAY·U - BOMBARDMENT
DAY·V - BOMBARDMENT
DAY·W· BOMBARDMENT/GAS
DAY·X· BOMBARDMENT/GAS
DAY·Y - BOMBARDMENT/GAS
DAY·Z - INFANTRY ASSAULT
A *FIVE*-DAY BOMBARDMENT? I SURE WOULDN'T WANT TO BE A GERMAN SOLDIER RIGHT NOW.
AND THIS, MY FELLOW SOLDIERS, IS WHY WE DUG OUR BUNKERS SO DEEP.
BOOOOOOOOM
WHEN THE SHELLING STOPS WE'LL HAVE PLENTY OF TIME TO EXIT THE BUNKERS, SET UP OUR MACHINE GUNS AND FIRE.
THE RAIDING PATROLS ARE BACK.
GIVE US YOUR REPORT.
SIR, WE SAW *NO OPENINGS* IN THE GERMAN WIRE.
WE SAW SOME GAPS WHERE TROOPS COULD ADANCE.
THE SHELLS HAD *NO EFFECT* ON THE WIRE IN OUR SECTOR.
JULY 1, 1916
LET'S GO SEE IF THERE ARE ANY GERMANS LEFT ALIVE. RIFLES AT THE READY! OVER THE TOP!
I THOUGHT THERE WOULD BE MORE *TANKS*.
ONLY A FEW EVEN MADE IT TO THE BATTLEFIELD.

TARGET THE BARBED WIRE. CUT A CLEAR PATH FOR OUR INFANTRY BOYS.
BOOM
BOOM
CLICK
ANOTHER DUD! THESE SHELLS ARE RUBBISH!
THERE IS NO NEED TO RUSH. THE ENEMY WILL HAVE TO CROSS TWENTY MILES OF OPEN GROUND TO GET TO US.
BOOOOOOOM
I WONDER HOW LONG THEY PLAN TO BOMBARD US.
DOES ANYONE HAVE ANY FOOD?
OUR SECTOR IS CLEAR OF WIRE.
OURS WAS YESTERDAY, BUT THE GERMANS PUT UP NEW WIRE.
WE HAVE TO SEND IN THE TROOPS—WE'RE ALREADY A DAY PAST SCHEDULE.
WE'VE HAD 'DAY-Y' TWICE NOW!
BARBED WIRE OR NO, IT'S TIME FOR THE INFANTRY ATTACK.
IT'S DAY-Z.
20,000 BRITISH SOLDIERS DIED ON THE FIRST DAY AT THE SOMME.

CHAPTER 28
LUDENDORFF AND HINDENBURG TAKE OVER
THEY ARE RUINING THIS MAP.
THE COORDINATED OFFENSE RAGED ALL SUMMER.
GERMANY
RUSSIA
AUSTRIA-HUNGARY
ROMANIA
SERBIA
BULGARIA
ITALY
OTTOMAN EMPIRE
THE BRITISH AT THE SOMME,
THE FRENCH AT VERDUN,
THE ITALIANS ON THE AUSTRIAN BORDER,
AND THE RUSSIANS AT GALICIA.
GENERAL VON FALKENHAYN, YOU WERE SUPPOSED TO BREAK THROUGH VERDUN IN A FEW WEEKS--IT'S BEEN MONTHS AND MONTHS!
YOU ARE RELIEVED OF DUTY!
IS THERE NO GENERAL WHO CAN LEAD US TO VICTORY?
WHAT ABOUT LUDENDORFF AND HINDENBURG?
BUT THEY ARE RUNNING THE EASTERN FRONT.
COULD THEY RUN BOTH FRONTS?
WHY NOT?
THEY WANT US TO GO BACK TO THE WESTERN FRONT.
THE AUSTRO-HUNGARIANS SHOULD BE ABLE TO HANDLE THE RUSSIANS NOW.
YOU'RE LEAVING US IN CHARGE?
YES. YOU WILL BE FINE. WE HAVE BROKEN THE SPIRIT OF THE RUSSIAN ARMY.
IF YOU ARE SURE...
WE ARE SURE!

CHAPTER 29
THE BRUSILOV OFFENSIVE
THEY THINK OUR SPIRIT IS BROKEN. IT ISN'T.
MOST OF THE GERMANS ARE LEAVING FOR THE WESTERN FRONT. WE HAVE FRESH SUPPLIES FROM OUR NEW ALLY, ROMANIA.
WE STRIKE HARD AND *FAST*!
NO MORE SLOW STEAMROLLER— NOW WE STRIKE LIKE LIGHTNING.
I ALMOST FEEL BAD FOR THOSE GRIFFINS.
WELL, YOU SHOULDN'T. THEY KICKED OFF THIS WHOLE MESS.
SHOCK TROOPERS *ADVANCE!*
THIS IS THEIR *WEAK POINT!*
BREAK THROUGH FOR **VICTORY!**
I THOUGHT WE'D BROKEN THEIR SPIRIT!
APPARENTLY NOT.
GENERAL BRUSILOV'S OFFENSIVE BROUGHT ABOUT RUSSIA'S GREATEST VICTORY IN WORLD WAR ONE--AND ONE OF THE DEADLIEST BATTLES IN *ALL OF HISTORY.*
EACH SIDE HAD OVER A MILLION CASUALTIES.
BY JOVE! I DIDN'T THINK THE RUSSIANS WOULD BE BACK.
NEITHER DID THE AUSTRO-HUNGARIANS, AND THEIR ARMY WAS SHATTERED FOR IT.

THERE WERE A MILLION CASUALTIES AT VERDUN AS WELL.
ATTACK! THE FORTRESS OF DOUAUMONT IS OURS AGAIN!
IT WAS THE SAME AT THE SOMME.
ON THE EASTERN FRONT, SO MANY SOLDIERS AND CIVILIANS DIED THERE WASN'T EVEN A CLEAR COUNT.

ONE SOLDIER, A FRENCH LIEUTENANT, WROTE IN HIS JOURNAL:
"HUMANITY IS MAD. IT MUST BE MAD TO DO WHAT IT IS DOING. WHAT A MASSACRE! WHAT SCENES OF HORROR AND CARNAGE! I CANNOT FIND WORDS TO TRANSLATE MY IMPRESSIONS.
HELL CANNOT BE SO TERRIBLE. MEN ARE MAD!"
1917
YIKES!

CHAPTER 30

THE NIVELLE OFFENSIVE

1917

THE TRENCHES REMAINED IN DEADLOCK.

ENGLAND'S NAVAL BLOCKADE HELD.

FOOD SHORTAGES SET IN.

U-BOATS CONTINUED TO SINK SUPPLY SHIPS.

THE WAR ROLLED ON.

HANG ON. I THOUGHT THE WAR METAPHOR WAS A BIG SCARY GOD WITH FOUR ARMS. WHAT'S THIS, A ROLLING SPIKED LOG?

RUN AWAY FROM THE SPIKY LOG, LITTLE PEOPLE!

I HAVE A PLAN TO WIN THIS WAR IN *48* HOURS. WE *ALL* ATTACK--

A *MILLION* AT ONCE--RIGHT THROUGH THE GERMAN LINE.

A MILLION TROOPS AND TWO HUNDRED TANKS!

×1,000,000

×200

VERY WELL, GENERAL NIVELLE. WE'LL TRY IT.

WE'LL PUSH THEM BACK-- ALL THE WAY BACK!

HUH? WHAT'S THAT?
THEY'VE BUILT A SET OF BACKUP TRENCHES!

HAH! WE EXPECTED AN ATTACK LIKE THIS!
WE SPENT ALL WINTER BUILDING OUR FALLBACK POSITIONS.

WE BROKE THEIR FRONT--WE CAN BREAK THIS SECOND LINE OF DEFENSE TOO.

THE BRITISH LED THE ATTACK WITH A MASSIVE BARRAGE.

CANADIAN TROOPS CHARGED AT VIMY--ONE OF THE STRONGEST GERMAN POSITIONS.
LOOK AT THAT. I RECKON WE'RE THE FIRST ALLIED SOLDIERS TO SEE THIS COUNTRY IN A YEAR!
THAT'S WHAT EVERYONE'S FIGHTING OVER, EH?
YUP, THAT'S IT.

THE FRENCH WEREN'T SO LUCKY. THE GERMAN LINE HELD FAST.
IT'S 1915 ALL OVER AGAIN. I CAN'T TAKE IT.
I HAVE HAD ENOUGH.

CHAPTER 31
THE BUNNIES
ON APRIL 6, 1917, SOMEBODY *NEW* JOINED THE WAR-- *THE AMERICANS.*
BUNNIES!
WHY THE CHANGE OF MIND NOW-- AFTER TWO AND A HALF *YEARS?*

WHEN THE *LUSITANIA* SANK, TEDDY ROOSEVELT, A FORMER U.S. PRESIDENT, SPOKE OUT FURIOUSLY AGAINST THE GERMANS.
THEY ARE NO BETTER THAN MURDERING **PIRATES**! WE SHOULD GO **TO WAR**!

WOODROW WILSON, THE CURRENT U.S. PRESIDENT, HAD OTHER PLANS.
THE UNITED STATES WILL **NOT** GO TO WAR.

AMERICAN AMMUNITION FACTORIES WERE SABOTAGED, BOMBS WERE PLANTED, A GERMAN SPY RING WAS CAPTURED-- STILL,
PRESIDENT WOODROW WILSON REMAINED FIRM.
WAR?
SPIES AMONG US?
BOMB SCARE!

"THERE WILL BE NO WAR. IT WOULD BE A CRIME AGAINST CIVILIZATION FOR US TO GO INTO IT."

THE AMERICAN PUBLIC HAD MIXED OPINIONS.
WE SHOULD GO FIGHT THOSE GERMANS!
I *AM* GERMAN!
I EMIGRATED TO AMERICA TO GET *AWAY* FROM THIS KIND OF TROUBLE.
I HOPE THEY FIGHT FOREVER. MY MUNITIONS FACTORY IS MAKING ME ***MILLIONS!***

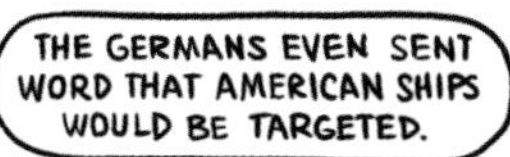
THE GERMANS EVEN SENT WORD THAT AMERICAN SHIPS WOULD BE TARGETED.

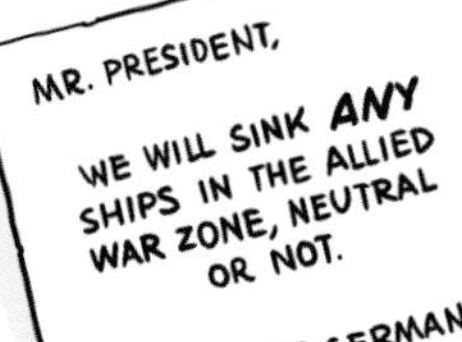
MR. PRESIDENT,

WE WILL SINK **ANY** SHIPS IN THE ALLIED WAR ZONE, NEUTRAL OR NOT.

THE GERMANS

THIS IS FOR SHOW.
THEY WON'T *REALLY* SINK OUR SHIPS.

THINK WE'RE BLUFFING?
JUST WATCH.

LOOK,
THREE AMERICAN MERCHANT SHIPS.
SINK THEM ALL.
IF WILSON DOESN'T GO TO WAR WITH GERMANY I WILL SKIN HIM ALIVE!
SIR, THE FOREIGN OFFICE HAS RECEIVED A STRANGE TELEGRAPH INTERCEPTION FROM BRITAIN.
WHAT IS IT?
IT'S FROM GERMANY TO... MEXICO.
THE ZIMMERMAN TELEGRAM
DEAR MEXICO,
WILL YOU BE OUR FRIEND?
IF YOU ATTACK THE UNITED STATES, WE WILL GIVE YOU MONEY AND WEAPONS. YOU CAN EVEN KEEP TEXAS, NEW MEXICO, ARIZONA, AND MAYBE EVEN KANSAS.
YOUR NEW BEST FRIEND, GERMANY
UNLIMITED SUBMARINE WARFARE, SINKING AMERICAN SHIPS, AND OFFERING FOUR AMERICAN STATES TO MEXICO!?
THAT'S IT! WE WILL GO TO WAR!
WONDERFUL NEWS! JUST BULLY!
"IT IS A FEARFUL THING TO LEAD THIS GREAT PEACEFUL PEOPLE INTO WAR, INTO THE MOST TERRIBLE AND DISASTROUS OF ALL WARS,
CIVILIZATION ITSELF SEEMING TO BE IN THE BALANCE. BUT THE RIGHT IS MORE PRECIOUS THAN PEACE."

LOOK AT ALL THOSE CHEERING BUNNIES.
THEY WON'T BE CHEERING WHEN THEY GET TO THE TRENCHES.
AMERICA HAD MANY WILLING MEN--
HURRY! SEND THEM OVER NOW!
QUICKLY! QUICKLY!
WE WILL ARRIVE WHEN WE ARE READY.
GENERAL PERSHING, WHEN WILL WE BE READY?
I'LL GO OVER NOW WITH A FEW ACTIVE TROOPS.
YOU MUST DO SO IN TOTAL SECRECY. GERMAN SPIES COULD ALERT THE U-BOATS.
YES, SIR.
WE'LL BE HOME FOR CHRISTMAS-- ONCE WE SORT OUT THOSE GERMANS!
BON VOYAGE!
GEN. PERSHING'S TOP SECRET WAR SUPPLIES FOR FRANCE
FRANCE
TOP SECRET
TOTAL SECRECY, HUH?

CHAPTER 32
THE BIG FOOOM
JUNE 7, 1917, MESSINES RIDGE, BELGIUM
TUNNELING LIKE RATS! RATS IN A HOLE IN YPRES!
I'D RATHER BE *UNDER* NO-MAN'S-LAND THAN OUT ON TOP OF IT.
I'VE BEEN ALIVE AND WELL, DIGGING SINCE 1915. YOU WON'T HEAR ME COMPLAINING.
SSSSH! WE ARE RIGHT UNDER THE GERMAN LINE.

SSSH! NOT A WORD--THE BRITISH WILL HEAR.
THOSE DOGS WILL NEVER EXPECT THIS!

IT'S COMPLETE.
TWO YEARS OF DIGGING, *TWENTY-ONE* TUNNELS--ALL PACKED TO THE BRIM WITH EXPLOSIVES.

IS EVERYONE OUT?
THE BIG DAY HAS ARRIVED.
TODAY WE BLOW THE TUNNELS.

CLICK

FOOOOOOOM
BLIMEY!
I BET THEY FELT THAT IN *LONDON*!
WE'RE CAPTURING THE GERMANS IN DROVES!
WE KNEW YOU WERE DOWN THERE. WE COULD HEAR YOU.
WE JUST DIDN'T KNOW YOU HAD THAT MUCH EXPLOSIVE.

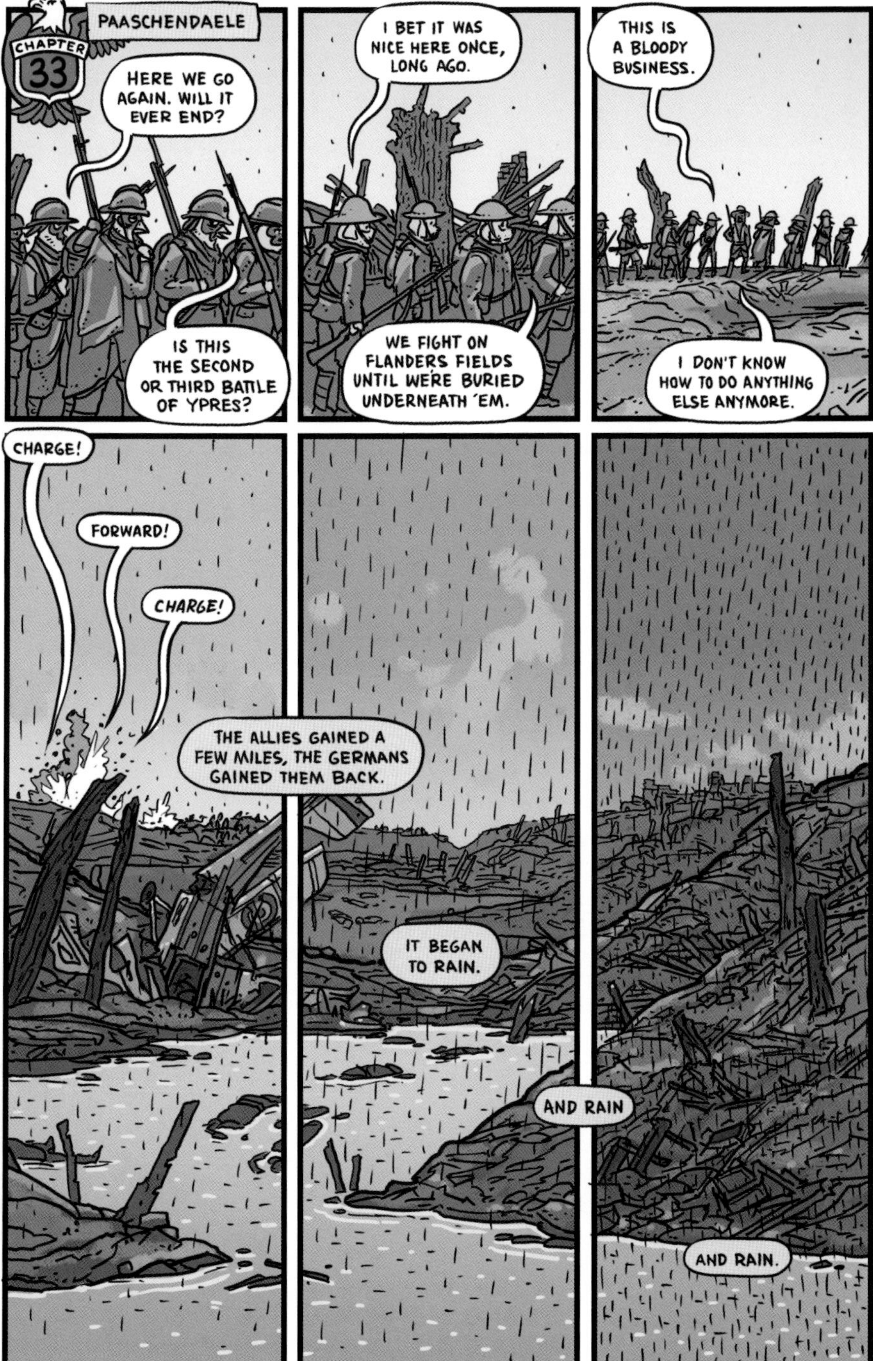
CHAPTER 33
PAASCHENDAELE
HERE WE GO AGAIN. WILL IT EVER END?
IS THIS THE SECOND OR THIRD BATTLE OF YPRES?
I BET IT WAS NICE HERE ONCE, LONG AGO.
WE FIGHT ON FLANDERS FIELDS UNTIL WE'RE BURIED UNDERNEATH 'EM.
THIS IS A BLOODY BUSINESS.
I DON'T KNOW HOW TO DO ANYTHING ELSE ANYMORE.
CHARGE!
FORWARD!
CHARGE!
THE ALLIES GAINED A FEW MILES, THE GERMANS GAINED THEM BACK.
IT BEGAN TO RAIN.
AND RAIN
AND RAIN.

WHEN THE RAIN CLEARED, THE ALLIES PUSHED FORWARD.
LOOK AT THAT. IT'S GREEN OVER THERE.
I SEE ACTUAL TREES.
THE RAIN HAD GONE, BUT THE MUD REMAINED.
CAREFUL. DON'T FALL OFF THEM DUCKBOARDS, YOU WON'T CLIMB OUT OF THAT MUD.
IT AIN'T JUST MUD, EITHER.

RIFLES JAMMED, THEIR WORKINGS CLOGGED WITH MUD.
COMBAT WAS OFTEN HAND-TO-HAND.

ON NOVEMBER 6, THE CANADIANS TOOK PAASCHENDAELE.
IS THIS IT? IS THIS THE TOWN?

JUST LOOKS LIKE A PILE OF BRICKS.

NOW HOLD ON A MINUTE·· WHERE ARE THE *BUNNIES*?
PERSHING AND HIS FORWARD GROUP ARRIVED IN ENGLAND IN JUNE. THIS WAS THE FIRST TIME AN AMERICAN ARMY HAD EVER APPEARED IN ENGLAND.

THE KING OF ENGLAND MET WITH GENERAL PERSHING.
IT HAS ALWAYS BEEN MY DREAM THAT THE TWO ENGLISH-SPEAKING NATIONS SHOULD SOMEDAY BE UNITED IN A GREAT CAUSE.
AND TODAY, MY DREAM IS REALIZED!
THERE YOU HAVE IT. ALLIES AND FRIENDS.
WELL, I'LL BE.

CHAPTER 34
THE BEAR REVOLUTION
I'M FROZEN, EXHAUSTED, AND OUT OF AMMO. EVERYONE I KNOW IS DEAD.
WE HAVE NEW PLANS! NEW WEAPONS FROM THE ALLIES--WE WILL RISE AGAIN!
I WON'T RISE AGAIN. I'M DONE.
I'M GOING HOME.
COME BACK HERE! YOU CAN'T JUST WALK AWAY!
THEY ARE JUST WALKING AWAY!
HUNDREDS OF THOUSANDS OF RUSSIAN SOLDIERS DESERTED THE FRONT LINES.
WHEN THEY REACHED THEIR HOMES, THEIR CITIES HAD CHANGED.
WHY IS EVERYONE MARCHING IN THE STREET?
THE PEOPLE OF RUSSIA, TIRED OF FOOD SHORTAGES, WAR, AND TERRIBLE CONDITIONS, BEGAN TO RISE UP AGAINST THE RUSSIAN ROYAL FAMILY.
NO MORE WAR!
MORE FOOD!
HEY! YEAH! I WANT MORE FOOD TOO! AND NO MORE WARS!
DOWN WITH THE TSAR!
DOWN WITH THE TSAR!

THE TSAR ABDICATED THE THRONE. THE ROMANOV FAMILY, WHO HAD RULED RUSSIA SINCE 1613, WAS OVERTHROWN.
THE TSAR AND HIS ENTIRE FAMILY WERE EXECUTED.
BY HANGING?
NO. ACTUALLY, THEY WERE GUNNED DOWN,
THEN STABBED,
THEN SHOT AT CLOSE RANGE.
COLD-BLOODED *BUTCHERY!*
THE RUSSIAN REVOLUTION HAD BEGUN.
THE ROYALS ARE DEAD! THE PEOPLE SHOULD RULE RUSSIA!
TROTSKY SHOULD BE IN CHARGE!
THE BOLSHEVIKS SHOULD BE IN CHARGE!
THE WORKERS SHOULD BE IN CHARGE!
THE *MILITARY* SHOULD BE IN CHARGE!
I SHOULD BE IN CHARGE.
(LENIN)
SOON THE RUSSIANS WERE BATTLING EACH OTHER.
LET'S OVERTHROW THE GOVERNMENT!
WE ALREADY DID THAT!
LET'S OVERTHROW THE *NEW* GOVERNMENT!
RUSSIA WAS FINISHED FIGHTING WORLD WAR ONE.
RUSSIA IS DONE! SEND EVERYONE TO THE WESTERN FRONT!
BOLSHEVIK REVOLUTION

CHAPTER 35
ASSEMBLY LINE
AS THE WAR GREW AND GREW, SO DID THE FACTORIES THAT MADE THE WAR MACHINES.

BIGGER GUNS! LONGER RANGE!
MORE SHELLS, MORE SHELLS!

BOMB THEIR FACTORIES! SEND OUT THE ZEPPELINS!

ZEPPELINS ARE AN EASY TARGET!

THE ALLIED PLANES SHOOT DOWN ALL OUR ZEPPELINS-- THEY'RE JUST TOO SLOW.
THEN SEND PLANES-- DROP BOMBS FROM PLANES!

GERMANY BEGAN USING A NEW WEAPON: THE STRATEGIC BOMBER PLANE.

THEY BOMBED LONDON AGAIN AND AGAIN.

BOMBER PLANES-- WE CAN BUILD THOSE TOO!
TARGET FACTORIES-- BLAST THEM TO BITS!

THE AIR WAR BECAME AS IMPORTANT AS THE BATTLES ON LAND AND SEA.
WE DON'T HAVE TIME TO COVER THE FLYING ACES OF WWI--THEIR ADVENTURES DESERVE A FULL BOOK.
AWW.

THIS GOD OF WAR METAPHOR HAS GOTTEN OUT OF CONTROL!

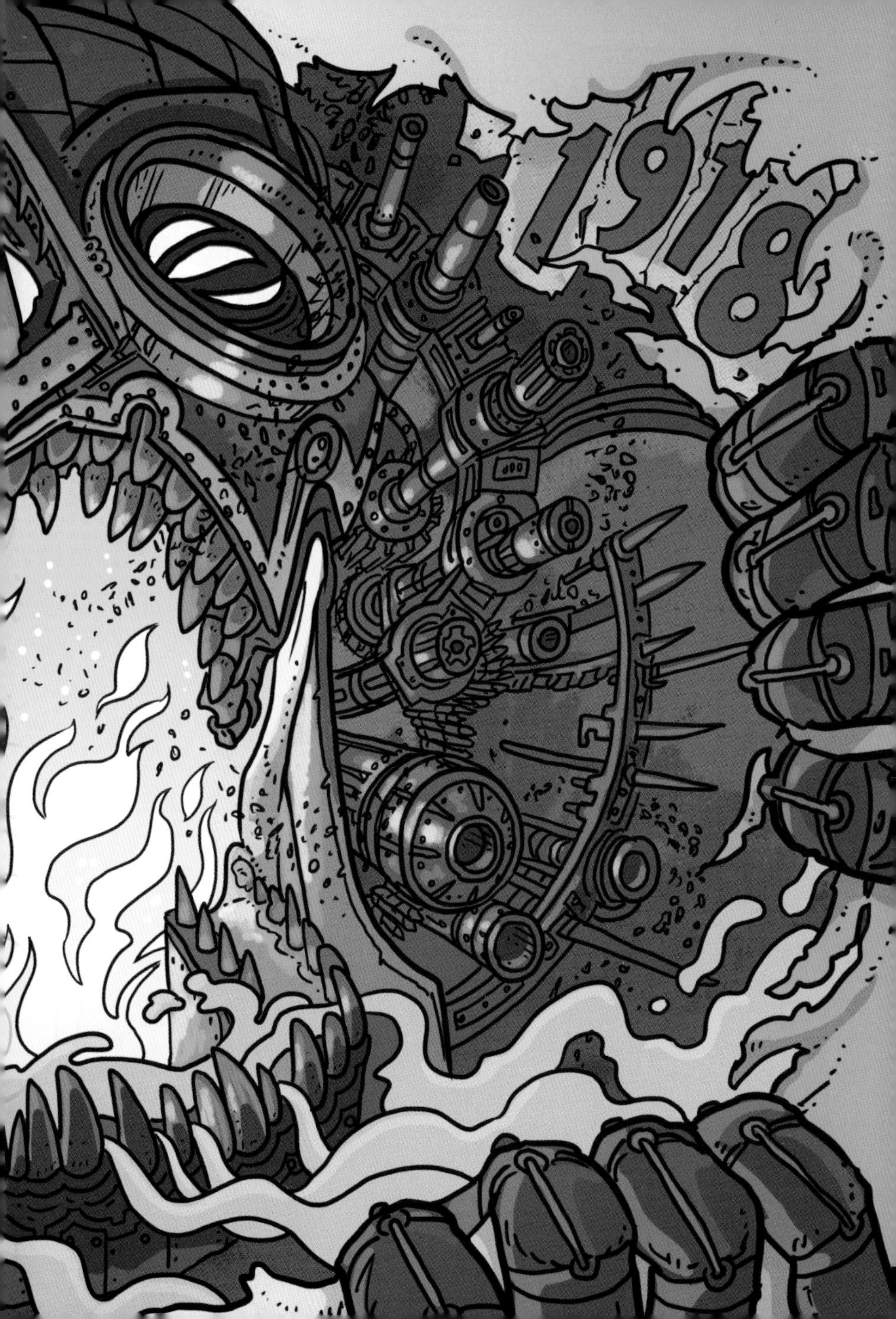
1918

CHAPTER 36
BORROWED HELMETS
ANOTHER YEAR? WHAT'S TAKING THE AMERICANS SO LONG?
I SUPPOSE IT TOOK A WHILE TO GET THEM ALL DRESSED.

THAT ACTUALLY *IS* PART OF THE REASON.
THE AMERICAN ARMY WAS SO LARGE, THERE WEREN'T ENOUGH GUNS, UNIFORMS, AND SUPPLIES TO GO AROUND.

BOYS, WHEN WE LAND, SEE THE BRITISH QUARTERMASTER TO GET A *RIFLE* AND ONE OF THOSE FUNNY LOOKIN' HELMETS.
WE'RE NOT USING *AMERICAN* GUNS?

THE LEE-ENFIELD IS A BRITISH RIFLE. BUT DON'T WORRY, SOME WERE MANUFACTURED IN AN AMERICAN FACTORY.

YOU MACHINE GUNNERS VISIT THE *FRENCH* QUARTERMASTER FOR YOUR FIREARMS.
La Mitrailleuse mode D'emploi
I CAN'T READ THESE FRENCH INSTRUCTIONS.
"Chauchat"

LOOK! REAL GRENADES!
I'VE NEVER SEEN LIVE ONES BEFORE.
WE TRAINED WITH POTATOES.

THEY AREN'T READY FOR BATTLE--THEY'VE NEVER SEEN GRENADES BEFORE!

WHEN WILL YOUR TROOPS BE READY TO SERVE UNDER BRITISH AND FRENCH COMMAND?
NEVER.
THESE TROOPS WILL ONLY FIGHT UNDER *MY* COMMAND.

WHAT!?
YOU HEARD ME. AMERICAN SOLDIERS WILL ONLY SERVE UNDER AMERICAN GENERALS.
IF YOU DON'T LIKE IT, TAKE IT UP WITH PRESIDENT WOODROW WILSON.

EVERYBODY ON THE TRAIN. WE'RE GOING TO A VILLAGE CALLED CANTIGNY.
ALL RIGHT, MEN, WE HAVE A MISSION: TO DESTROY A GERMAN SALIENT.
GREAT! WHAT'S A SALIENT?
A SALIENT IS A BUBBLE IN THE LINE WHERE THE GERMAN TRENCH BULGES OUT.
SALIENT
THIS IS THE FIRST AMERICAN OFFENSIVE HERE IN FRANCE. DON'T MESS IT UP.
MAY 28, 1918
CANTIGNY, FRANCE
BOY, THAT'S LOUD!
SEEMS LIKE WE'VE BEEN SHELLING THEM FOR HOURS. HOW LONG HAS IT BEEN?
15 MINUTES. THIS WILL BE A ONE-HOUR BARRAGE.
THEN WE CHARGE IN AND MOP UP!
RIGHT.
I'M STICKING BY PRIVATE JUAN--HE'S MY GOODLUCK CHARM.
WHY?
HAVEN'T YOU HEARD? PRIVATE JUAN WAS ON THE SS TUSCANIA--
THE TROOP CARRIER THAT GOT TORPEDOED?
YUP. IF HE SURVIVED THAT, HE CAN SURVIVE ANYTHING.
RIGHT, JUAN?
I SURE HOPE SO.

OKAY, BOYS! THAT'S IT. OVER THE TOP!
MAKE FOR THE VILLAGE!

45 MINUTES LATER
THE VILLAGE OF CANTIGNY IS SECURE.
WE WON!
HOORAY FOR THE AMERICAN EXPEDITIONARY FORCE!

WE DID IT!
WE WON OUR FIRST BATTLE!

WHERE'S PRIVATE JUAN?
HE DIDN'T MAKE IT. HE WAS GUNNED DOWN IN THE BATTLE.

200 AMERICAN SOLDIERS DIED IN THE BATTLE OF CANTIGNY. INCLUDING PRIVATE MATHEW B. JUAN, FROM ARIZONA, OF THE PIMA TRIBE.

CHAPTER 37

CHEMIN-DES-DAMES

IT'S SO PEACEFUL HERE.
IT WAS AWFULLY NICE OF THE GENERALS TO PUT US IN SUCH A QUIET PART OF THE LINE.
HUH?
GAS AND STORM TROOPERS!
STORM TROOPERS AND GAS!
TELL GENERAL HINDENBURG WE HAVE BROKEN THROUGH THE LINE AT CHEMIN-DES-DAMES AND ADVANCED FIFTEEN MILES.
THE GENERAL WILL BE HAPPY TO HEAR IT!
FORWARD, MARCH!
WE DON'T STOP UNTIL WE SEE THE EIFFEL TOWER.
HALT! ENEMY TROOPS AHEAD!
HOLD POSITIONS, WAIT FOR THE BOMBARDMENT.
WHAT IF THEY DON'T DO A BOMBARDMENT?
THE FRENCH AND ENGLISH *ALWAYS* DO A BOMBARDMENT.

ATTACK!
LOOK AT THEM GO!
HUZZAH FOR THE BUNNIES!
DON'T CALL US BUNNIES--
CALL US *DOUGHBOYS*.
THEY DIDN'T DO A BOMBARDMENT.

CHAPTER 38
THE MARINES IN BELLEAU WOOD
THE GERMANS HAVE BROKEN THE LINE NEAR CHÂTEAU-THIERRY!
SHOW US THE WAY. WE CAN FILL THAT HOLE. WE'LL MARCH THROUGH THE NIGHT IF WE HAVE TO!
DIG IN WITH BAYONETS. WE'LL SURPRISE THEM.
ADVANCE!
WAIT TILL THEY'RE CLOSER.
CLOSER...
FIRE!
AAAGH! RETREAT! INTO THE WOODS!
LET'S GO IN THERE AND GET THEM!
NO, THEY ARE TOO WELL POSITIONED. WE SHOULD RETREAT.
RETREAT? HELL, WE JUST GOT HERE!
THE MARINES MARCHED INTO BELLEAU WOOD.
ACTUAL WWI QUOTE FROM MAJOR LLOYD W. WILLIAMS
FOR TWENTY-SIX DAYS, THE MARINES FOUGHT THROUGH THE FOREST.
8,000 MARINES WERE WOUNDED. 1,811 WERE KILLED.
BUT THEY TOOK BELLEAU WOOD.

CHAPTER 39

A BLACK DAY

LUDENDORFF AND HINDENBURG HAVE USED UP THEIR SPRING OFFENSIVE.
THEY GAINED SOME GROUND, BUT THEY LOST A LOT OF MEN.

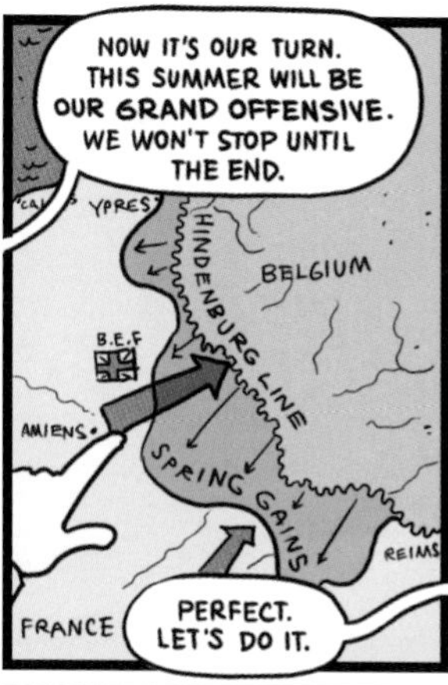

NOW IT'S OUR TURN. THIS SUMMER WILL BE OUR **GRAND OFFENSIVE**. WE WON'T STOP UNTIL THE END.
YPRES
HINDENBURG LINE
BELGIUM
B.E.F
AMIENS
SPRING GAINS
REIMS
FRANCE
PERFECT. LET'S DO IT.

AUGUST 8, 1918
AMIENS, FRANCE
THE ALLIES BROUGHT EVERYTHING IN THEIR ARSENAL.

HEAVY BRITISH MARK V TANKS,

LITTLE WHIPPET TANKS,

LIGHT FRENCH RENAULT TANKS

--OVER **500** TANKS IN ALL.

WHAT A SIGHT TO **BEHOLD**! SO MANY **TANKS**!

YOU'RE WELCOME.

THIS WALL OF WEAPONS ERASED MOST OF THE GROUND GERMANY HAD GAINED IN THEIR SPRING OFFENSIVE.

CANADIAN TROOPS ADVANCED SO QUICKLY, THEY CAPTURED SOME GERMANS STILL EATING BREAKFAST.
HUH? CANADIANS?
SURRENDER!
YES! YES! WE SURRENDER TO *CANADA*!
DID YOU BRING ANY MAPLE SYRUP?

VICTORY! VICTORY AT AMIENS! HOORAY FOR THE GRAND OFFENSIVE!

THIS IS A BLACK DAY FOR GERMANY.

CHAPTER 40
PRICKLY PERSHING
GENERAL PERSHING, YOUR AMERICAN TROOPS WILL MARCH SOUTH OF VERDUN TO TAKE THE FORTRESS OF METZ.

I CAN DO THAT. I HAVE 500,000 TROOPS, READY TO MARCH.
MAGNIFIQUE!
OUR REPORTS SAY FEWER THAN 25,000 GERMANS HOLD THE FORT.

NO, NO, NO-- LET THE GERMANS *KEEP* METZ. IT HAS LITTLE STRATEGIC VALUE.
BUT--

I WANT THE AMERICANS SPREAD OUT, SUPPORTING THE FRENCH AND BRITISH ALONG THE MEUSE IN THE ARGONNE FOREST.

GENERAL FOCH, I DON'T WANT TO BE RUDE, BUT MY AMERICAN ARMY IS *INDEPENDENT!*
WE DIDN'T COME HERE TO BE *SUPPORT UNITS*!
DID YOU COME TO HELP US OR **NOT**!?

WE'LL MARCH AS AN AMERICAN ARMY UNIT OR NOT AT ALL!
GENERAL PERSHING, I **MUST INSIST**!
WHOA! THEY'RE GONNA FIGHT!

WHY IS GENERAL PERSHING BEING SO DIFFICULT?
SOUNDS LIKE *NATIONALISM* TO ME.
PERSHING HAD STRONG OPINIONS ABOUT WHAT WAS BEST FOR HIS TROOPS.

GENERALS, PLEASE. LET'S NOT FIGHT.
WHAT IF YOU DO *BOTH*-- ATTACK METZ, THEN GO TO THE MEUSE-ARGONNE.

YEAH. I COULD DO THAT. MY BOYS COULD DO *BOTH*, NO PROBLEM.
SEE? THAT'S BETTER. ALLIES ARE SUPPOSED TO GET ALONG.

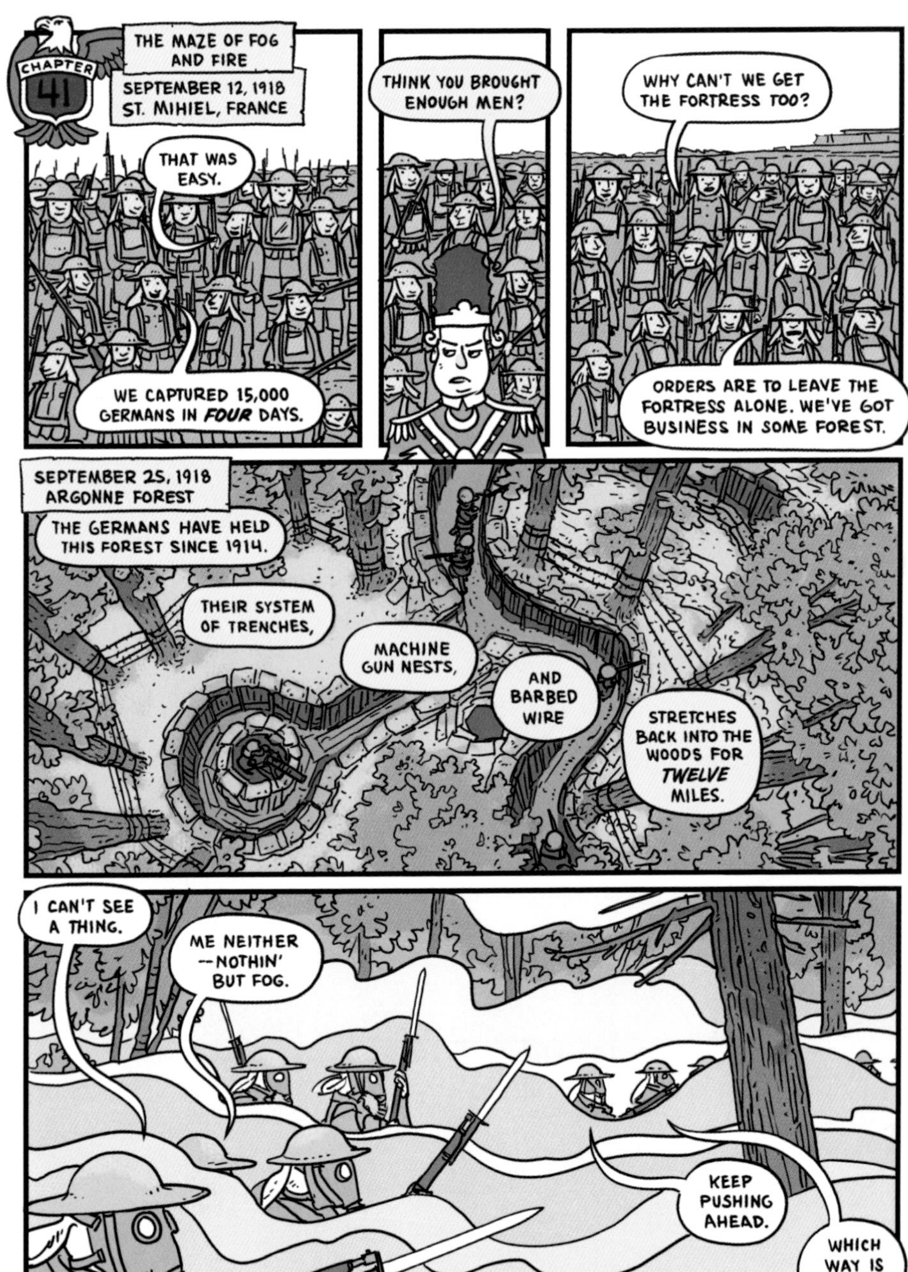
CHAPTER 41
THE MAZE OF FOG AND FIRE
SEPTEMBER 12, 1918
ST. MIHIEL, FRANCE
THAT WAS EASY.
WE CAPTURED 15,000 GERMANS IN *FOUR* DAYS.
THINK YOU BROUGHT ENOUGH MEN?
WHY CAN'T WE GET THE FORTRESS TOO?
ORDERS ARE TO LEAVE THE FORTRESS ALONE. WE'VE GOT BUSINESS IN SOME FOREST.
SEPTEMBER 25, 1918
ARGONNE FOREST
THE GERMANS HAVE HELD THIS FOREST SINCE 1914.
THEIR SYSTEM OF TRENCHES,
MACHINE GUN NESTS,
AND BARBED WIRE
STRETCHES BACK INTO THE WOODS FOR *TWELVE* MILES.
I CAN'T SEE A THING.
ME NEITHER --NOTHIN' BUT FOG.
KEEP PUSHING AHEAD.
WHICH WAY IS AHEAD?

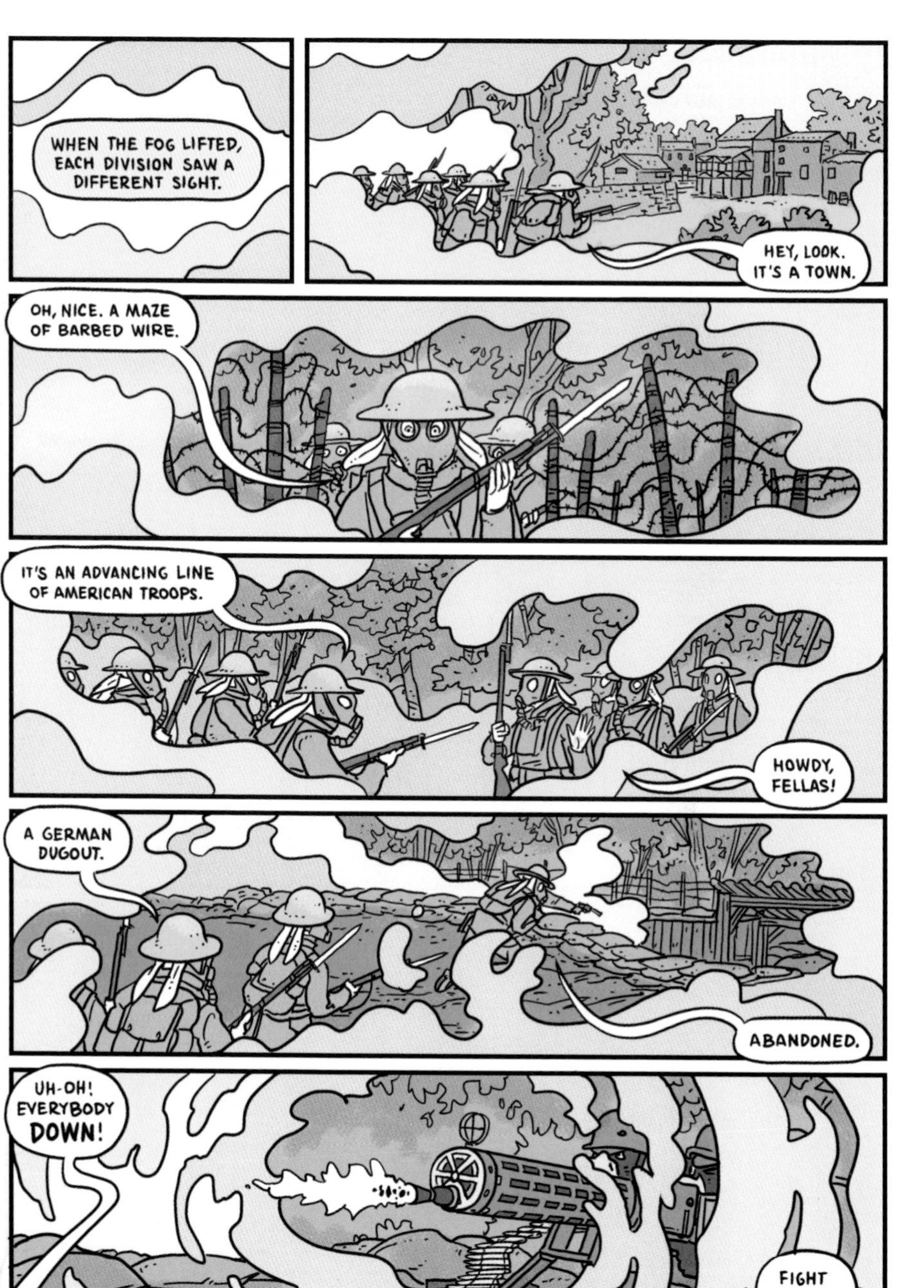
WHEN THE FOG LIFTED, EACH DIVISION SAW A DIFFERENT SIGHT.
HEY, LOOK. IT'S A TOWN.
OH, NICE. A MAZE OF BARBED WIRE.
IT'S AN ADVANCING LINE OF AMERICAN TROOPS.
HOWDY, FELLAS!
A GERMAN DUGOUT.
ABANDONED.
UH-OH! EVERYBODY **DOWN**!
FIGHT FOR IT!

ONE TROOP, THE 33RD PRAIRIE DIVISION FROM ILLINOIS, FOUND THEMSELVES DEEP IN A SWAMP.
I GUESS WE HAVE TO CROSS.
YOU CAN'T CROSS HERE--IT'S IMPASSABLE.

I DON'T SEE ANY GERMANS. MAYBE THEY THINK IT'S IMPASSABLE TOO.
I THINK WE CAN DO IT.

MARK ANY ROUTE THAT WORKS WITH TAPE.
WE'LL GET ACROSS.

KEEP MOVIN'! MY ARMS ARE GETTIN' SORE.

DO WE HAVE TO SLEEP HERE IN THE MUCK?
I GUESS WE DO.

STEP BY STEP,
DAY BY DAY,
THE AMERICANS CROSSED THE ARGONNE.

THIS RAVINE IS THE ONLY ROUTE THROUGH.
IT'S FULL OF SKELETONS.

YES, FRENCH SKELETONS. IT'S THE ONLY ROUTE.
36
36

OKAY. I HOPE THE GERMANS HOLDING THE RAVINE ARE **GONE**.
GET IT--*"ARE GONE"*? ARGONNE!

TWO HUNDRED SOLDIERS FROM THE 114TH DIVISION, NEW JERSEY, WENT INTO THE RAVINE.
THIRTEEN CAME OUT.
ANOTHER GROUP, THE 77TH "STATUE OF LIBERTY" DIVISION, WENT TOO FAR ALTOGETHER.
WHERE IS EVERYONE?
SEND OUT PATROLS-- CHECK WITH OUR SUPPORT DIVISIONS ON EITHER SIDE.
PATROLS ARE BACK. WE HAVE NO SUPPORT ON EITHER SIDE.
IN FACT, WE'RE SURROUNDED BY GERMANS.
HOLD TIGHT AND DIG IN.
WE'LL FIGHT 'EM OFF UNTIL OUR SUPPORT TROOPS DO ARRIVE.
INCOMING!
THOSE AREN'T GERMAN SHELLS! THOSE ARE OURS!
WE'RE BEING SHELLED BY OUR OWN GUYS!

WE'VE GOT TO GET WORD TO THEM BEFORE THEY BLOW US TO BITS!
WHAT COMMUNICATIONS DO WE HAVE?
WE'VE GOT HOMING PIGEONS.
SEND A PIGEON!
We are along the road parallel 276.4 our artillery is dropping a barrage directly on us. For heaven's sake, STOP IT.
FLY, LITTLE GUY.
BANG
THIS IS GREAT! AN ANIMAL STORY INSIDE AN ANIMAL STORY!
WHAT HAPPENED, D THEY SHOOT HIM?
SECOND BIRD, AWAY.
I CAN'T WATCH!
THE GERMANS ARE SHOOTING ALL OUR PIGEONS!

THIS IS OUR LAST PIGEON.
GOOD LUCK, DEAR FRIEND.
HEY, THAT'S HIS NAME, *CHER AMI*-- THAT MEANS "DEAR FRIEND".
GOOD LUCK, CHER AMI. WE'RE ALL COUNTING ON YOU.
KEEP FLAPPING CHER AMI! YOU CAN DO IT!
BANG
BANG
BANG
WE'LL KNOW HE MADE IT IF THE ARTILLERY STOPS.
I HOPE HE MAKES IT!
LISTEN... IT STOPPED.
HE MADE IT! THAT LITTLE PIGEON SAVED THE DAY!

CHAPTER
42
11/11 AT 11:00
THE ARGONNE IS FULL OF AMERICANS!
THEY SEND MORE TROOPS EVERY DAY!

WHERE ARE OUR REINFORCEMENTS?
TELL THE AUSTRO-HUNGARIANS TO SEND FRESH TROOPS.
ER... BAD NEWS FROM AUSTRIA-HUNGARY.

THE EMPIRE OF AUSTRIA-HUNGARY SURRENDERS.
DO WE EVEN HAVE AN EMPIRE ANYMORE?

THEN GET TROOPS FROM THE OTTOMAN EMPIRE!
UM...

WE GIVE UP. THE OTTOMAN EMPIRE SURRENDERS.

WE JUST NEED A FEW MORE MEN TO HOLD OUR LINE-- BULGARIA?

BULGARIA HAS SURRENDERED.

WE ARE ALONE, THE LAST OF THE CENTRAL POWERS.
WE CAN'T WIN.

HAVE THE LEAVES FALLEN YET?
YES, FOR THE FIFTH TIME.

ON NOVEMBER 9, 1918, THE KAISER ABDICATED THE GERMAN THRONE.
GOOD-BYE, EVERYONE.
THE WORLD'S LEADERS BEGAN TO TALK ABOUT *ARMISTICE*.
WHAT'S ARMISTICE MEAN?
IT MEANS *PEACE*.
THE ARMISTICE WAS SIGNED. EVERYONE AGREED:
ON NOVEMBER 11, AT 11:00, THE GUNS WOULD STOP.
THE LAST BATTLES WERE STILL BEING FOUGHT.
DID YOU HEAR, LADS? THE ARMISTICE IS TODAY!
THE WAR ENDS AT 11:00!
DO THE GERMANS KNOW?
WE'LL SOON FIND OUT. IT'S 10:58.
RATATATATATATA
10:59...
RATATATATAT
11:00 ON THE NOSE.
·CLICK·

BOOM BOOM BOOM BOOM BOOM BOOM BOOM BOOM BOOM BOOM BOOM BOOM BOOM

WAR WAS STOPPED, DISMANTLED, AND PACKED AWAY.
WAR
DANGER
ITS ALL-CONSUMING RAMPAGE WAS OVER.
WAR
DEPARTMENT

JUST LIKE THAT?
JUST LIKE THAT.

THERE IS NO GOD OF WAR.
WAR IS BUILT AND CONTROLLED BY HUMAN HANDS-- HUMANS START IT, HUMANS STOP IT.

THEN WHY DIDN'T THEY STOP IT EARLIER-- BEFORE IT KILLED EVERYBODY!?!

WHY DID THEY LET IT OUT IN THE FIRST PLACE!?
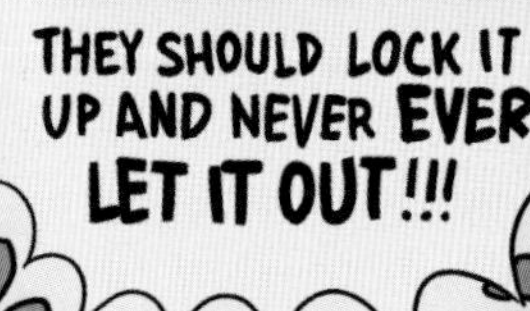

THEY SHOULD LOCK IT UP AND NEVER EVER LET IT OUT!!!

CALM DOWN, HANGMAN! THERE ARE TIMES WHEN WAR IS A NECESSITY.
TELL HIM IT IS SO, CAPTAIN HALE.

I'M NOT HERE TO JUDGE WHICH WARS WERE NECESSARY AND WHICH WARS WEREN'T. I JUST TELL THE STORY.
WORLD WAR ONE IS BEST SUMMED UP BY THOSE WHO EXPERIENCED IT.

"WORLD WAR I WAS THE MOST COLOSSAL, MURDEROUS, MISMANAGED BUTCHERY THAT HAS EVER TAKEN PLACE ON EARTH."

-ERNEST HEMINGWAY
AN AMBULANCE DRIVER ON THE ITALIAN FRONT

"ANYONE WHO SAYS HE ENJOYS THIS KIND OF THING IS EITHER A LIAR OR A MADMAN."

-CAPTAIN HARRY YOXALL

"ONE HAS INDEED PERSONALLY TO COME UNDER THE SHADOW OF WAR TO FEEL FULLY ITS OPPRESSION...

BY 1918, ALL BUT ONE OF MY CLOSE FRIENDS WERE DEAD."

- 2ND LIEUTENANT
J.R.R. TOLKIEN

"IN WAR THERE IS NO PLACE FOR A GOD OF LOVE, NO TIME FOR THE SOFTER EMOTIONS, AND NO INCLINATION TO WORRY ABOUT A FUTURE WHEN THE PRESENT IS A HELL THAT THE DEVIL HIMSELF WOULD BE PROUD TO REIGN OVER."

-PRIVATE J. BOWLES

"THE WAR WAS DECIDED IN THE FIRST TWENTY DAYS OF FIGHTING, AND ALL THAT HAPPENED AFTERWARDS CONSISTED IN BATTLES WHICH, HOWEVER FORMIDABLE AND DEVASTATING, WERE BUT DESPARATE AND VAIN APPEALS AGAINST THE DECISION OF FATE."

-WINSTON CHURCHILL

"ALL WAR IS A SYMPTOM OF MAN'S FAILURE AS A THINKING ANIMAL."

-JOHN STEINBECK

MR. STEINBECK DID NOT SERVE IN WWI— HE WAS IN HIGH SCHOOL IN 1918. BUT HIS QUOTE IS PERFECT FOR OUR BOOK.

IT SURE IS.

IT WAS CALLED THE WAR TO END ALL WARS.
WAS IT? DID IT END ALL WARS?
NO. IT DIDN'T.
BUT IT *CHANGED* ALL WARS.
MEN RODE IN ON HORSES...
AND RODE OUT IN TANKS.
THESE WEAPONS...
BECAME THESE WEAPONS.
THIS...
BECAME THIS.

IT CHANGED THE WORLD TOO.
THIS...
BECAME THIS.
SOME NEW LINES WERE DRAWN ON THE MAP.
RUSSIA
GERMANY
AUSTRIA-HUNGARY
SERBIA
ROMANIA
OTTOMAN EMPIRE
THESE COUNTRIES...
TURNED INTO THESE COUNTRIES.
U.S.S.R
ESTONIA
LATVIA
LITHUANIA
EAST PRUSSIA
POLAND
CZECHOSLOVAKIA
GERMANY
AUSTRIA
HUNGARY
ROMANIA
YUGOSLAVIA
TURKEY
SOME EMPIRES DISAPPEARED.
FIFTEEN MILLION SOLDIERS...
CAME HOME INJURED, BLIND, MAIMED OR SHELL-SHOCKED.
NINE MILLION SOLDIERS...
NEVER CAME HOME AT ALL.

THAT IS THE STORY OF THE GREAT WAR-- WITH ANIMALS WEARING HATS.

I'M A LITTLE DIZZY.
THAT WAS A LOT OF WAR TO TAKE IN.

THE HANGMAN IS NOT WRONG. THAT WAS A STAGGERING CONFLICT.

THAT WAS JUST A QUICK OVER-VIEW--WE SKIPPED MANY ASPECTS OF THE WAR ENTIRELY:
THE MIDDLE EAST,
THE BATTLE FOR AIR SUPREMACY,
THE INFLUENZA EPIDEMIC,
THE ARMENIAN GENOCIDE--
GIVE US A REST!
HEY NOW! YOU SAID THE STORY WAS OVER.

THE 20TH CENTURY SOUNDS TERRIBLE!

FOR YOUR NEXT TALE, I'D LIKE A NICE STORY, WHERE NOBODY GETS SHOT, GASSED, EXPLODED, OR BAYONETED.
BUT KEEP THE ANIMALS--AND THE HATS.

SO...
GOLDILOCKS AND THE THREE BEARS?
OOH, YES! YES!
I'D ENJOY THAT!
OKAY, BUT AFTER THAT, WE'RE GOING RIGHT BACK TO HISTORY TALES.

ONCE UPON A TIME, THERE WAS A LITTLE GIRL NAMED GOLDILOCKS.
DID SHE HAVE CURLY BLOND HAIR!?
THE CURLIEST...

NH
HT
NATHAN
HALE'S
HAZARDOUS
TALES

BIBLIOGRAPHY

BOOKS

THE FIRST WORLD WAR: A VERY SHORT INTRODUCTION
MICHAEL HOWARD
OXFORD UNIVERSITY PRESS, 2002

A WORLD UNDONE: THE STORY OF THE GREAT WAR
G.J. MEYER
BANTAM DELL, 2006

THE GUNS OF AUGUST
BARBARA W. TUCHMAN
RANDOM HOUSE, 1962

TO CONQUER HELL: THE MEUSE-ARGONNE, 1918
EDWARD G. LENGEL
HENRY HOLT AND COMPANY, 2008

LOST BATTALIONS: THE GREAT WAR AND THE CRISIS OF AMERICAN NATIONALITY
RICHARD SLOTKIN
HENRY HOLT AND COMPANY, 2005

A STORM IN FLANDERS: THE YPRES SALIENT, 1914-1918
WINSTON GROOM
ATLANTIC MONTHLY PRESS, 2002

BOOKS WITH LOTS OF PICTURES

WORLD WAR I IN CARTOONS
MARK BRYANT
GRUB STREET PUBLISHING, 2006

AN ILLUSTRATED ENCYCLOPEDIA OF UNIFORMS OF WORLD WAR I
JONATHAN NORTH AND JEREMY BLACK
ANNESS PUBLISHING, 2012

AN ILLUSTRATED HISTORY OF THE FIRST WORLD WAR
JOHN KEEGAN
KNOPF, 2001

THE WAR TO END ALL WARS: WORLD WAR I
RUSSELL FREEDMAN
CLARION BOOKS, 2010

VIDEO

THE GREAT WAR
26-EPISODE DOCUMENTARY
BBC, 1964

COMICS (NOT KID FRIENDLY)

IT WAS THE WAR OF THE TRENCHES
JACQUES TARDI
FANTAGRAPHICS, 2010

GODDAMN THIS WAR!
JACQUES TARDI, JEAN-PIERRE VERNEY
FANTAGRAPHICS, 2013

UM. HEY, CORRECTION BABY, WHERE ARE THE HISTORICAL PORTRAITS THAT ARE SUPPOSED TO BE HERE?
Don't need them.

WHAT!? WE *DO* NEED THEM!
THINK OF ALL THE GENERALS! THE *KINGS, KAISERS, TSARS, DUKES, AND ARCHDUKES!*

They all look like this.
CB
Old white man with big mustache.

YOU AREN'T WRONG.

BUT WE REALLY NEED A PHOTO OF SOMETHING FROM WORLD WAR I.

Too bad. No photo.

HOLD ON. I THINK I HAVE A PHOTO ON MY PHONE.

THIS IS A PHOTO I TOOK OF *CHER AMI,* THE HERO PIGEON. HE CAN BE SEEN AT THE SMITHSONIAN'S NATIONAL MUSEUM OF AMERICAN HISTORY.

That's a good photo. Dead bird is better than old mustache man.

HAVE A QUESTION, COMMENT, OR CORRECTION? SEND IT TO OUR OWN CORRECTION BABY.

CORRECTIONBABY@
HAZARDOUSTALES.COM

THAT'S A NICE-LOOKING TURTLE-BANGER YOU GOT THERE.

PHOTO: BARBARA BRAND

AUTHOR/ILLUSTRATOR NATHAN HALE AT THE *NATIONAL WORLD WAR I MUSEUM AT LIBERTY MEMORIAL*, KANSAS CITY, MISSOURI. BEHIND HIM IS A *RENAULT FT-17* TANK.

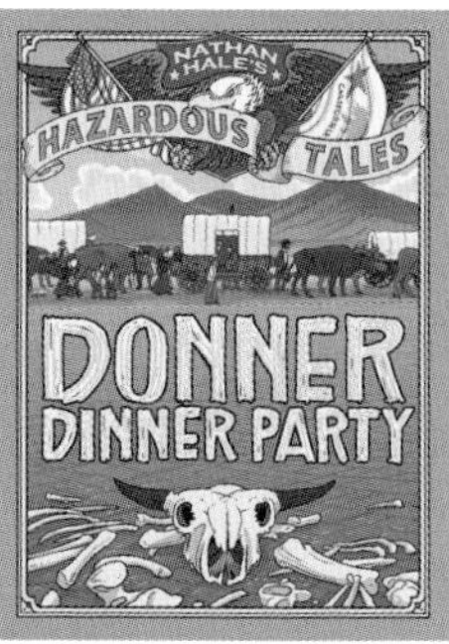

ATLANTIC OCEAN
NORWAY
SCOTLAND
NORTH SEA
DENMARK
IRELAND
GREAT BRITAIN
WALES
LUSITANIA SUNK 1915
NETHERLANDS
ENGLAND
N
W
E
S
BELGIUM
GERMANY
WESTERN FRONT
SWITZ.
FRANCE
ITALIAN FRONT
PORTUGAL
ITALY
SPAIN
MEDITERRANEAN SEA